# THE NEXT STEP IN EVOLUTION
## —A PERSONAL GUIDE

# The Next Step in Evolution
## —A Personal Guide

▼

*Vincent Cole*

Writers Club Press
San Jose  New York  Lincoln  Shanghai

The Next Step in Evolution—A Personal Guide

All Rights Reserved © 2000 by Vincent Cole

No part of this book may be reproduced or transmitted in any form or by any means, graphic, electronic, or mechanical, including photocopying, recording, taping, or by any information storage retrieval system, without the permission in writing from the publisher.

Writers Club Press
an imprint of iUniverse.com, Inc.

For information address:
iUniverse.com, Inc.
5220 S 16th, Ste. 200
Lincoln, NE 68512
www.iuniverse.com

ISBN: 0-595-15513-8

Printed in the United States of America

# Epigraph

▼

*"Do not imagine that the journey is short; one must have the heart of a lion to follow this unusual road for it is as long as the sea is deep. One plods along in a state of amazement, sometimes smiling, sometimes weeping."* —Attar

# Acknowledgements

▼

Cover Design by Michael Carnahan and Vincent Cole
Edited by Donna McDonough

# CONTENTS

Introduction .................................................................. 1
To the Readers of this Simple Message ......................... 5
Chapter 1    The Next Step ........................................... 7
Chapter 2    The Ego .................................................. 12
Chapter 3    Begin the Journey .................................. 21
Chapter 4    Beyond the Ego ...................................... 26
Chapter 5    A Simple Experiment ............................. 38
Chapter 6    Conflict ................................................... 48
Chapter 7    Serving Two Masters .............................. 53
Chapter 8    The Power of Decision ........................... 60
Chapter 9    Strength .................................................. 69
Chapter 10   Intellect .................................................. 77
Chapter 11   Knowledge .............................................. 82
Chapter 12   Wisdom ................................................... 86
Chapter 13   Trust ....................................................... 90

| | | |
|---|---|---|
| Chapter 14 | Forgiveness | 96 |
| Chapter 15 | Compassion | 105 |
| Chapter 16 | A Gift For Your Soul | 110 |
| Chapter 17 | A Reminder | 116 |
| Chapter 18 | Discipline and Patience | 121 |
| Chapter 19 | Peace | 126 |
| Chapter 20 | The Limits of Love | 131 |
| Chapter 21 | Divine Love | 137 |
| Chapter 22 | The Beginning | 144 |

# Introduction

▼

"What is important is the message, not the messenger."

Those words were spoken by one of many voices channeled through an individual affectionately called "Our Host," and more often, "Our Friend." Each of the voices had a distinct personality. Some even spoke with an accent. While presenting the message of this book they would laugh, gesture, shout at times, and when needed, depart from dictation to give someone personal attention. On some occasions they would place a hand on a body that was sick or a mind that was troubled. No words were spoken. No message was given, only comfort and healing.

Who were they? Who were these voices, these distinct personalities who joined with a human body to teach, to cajole, and to sometimes even scold the small group of listeners gathering twice a week to hear the next part of the message?

When asked who they were the reply was always the same: "We are servants. We have come to serve you, to help you."

Once they were asked, "Where do you come from?"

They answered with a smile, "The same place as you. We come from God."

We. They always said we, no matter which of the several teachers were talking. Rarely did any one of them talk about himself or herself as an individual, and then it was only to illustrate a point they were trying to make. Instead, they encouraged those who would listen to also think in terms of we or us, to go beyond the individual self and expand our awareness to include others. The word "I" separates you, they would say. Try to be more inclusive. Try to think of yourself as something greater than your individual body. We tried. We continue to try.

For several months we listened as the message was given. We got used to seeing one teacher appear, give a chapter or two then step aside so that another could take the dictation to another level. It is true that some who sat in on the sessions did not believe in what they saw and heard. They did not believe that personalities outside a physical body could exist and while many left, a few did remain in spite of their disbelief.

There were others, however, who began to notice how events in their lives were in synchronization with the dictation. When the teachers spoke of spiritual nature of conflict, they were experiencing great conflict. When the message was on the need for strength, those same people were feeling weak and overwhelmed. And, when the chapter was on forgiveness, the same groups of people were suddenly having memories of past sorrow and pain. Those people were living the message. Still, there were some parts of the message that weren't so easily understood. We would discuss it afterwards, wondering if certain words were true.

"It is not enough to just hear the words," they told us. "You must live them." It takes time; they would remind us. Be patient.

At the end of the dictation they asked us to do nothing more with the information until we were ready, until we had a better understanding. Years passed. Now and then one of the servants would again appear like an old friend. Sometimes a new servant appeared. They came to help an individual, add to the message previously given, or offer guidance to their "dear friend," the host through whom they spoke.

Then it was time. While on a yearlong retreat in the desert, we took the manuscript from its dusty box. While coyotes sang at night and rattlesnakes sought shade during the day, the message took its final form.

Additional information was given. The servants returned to finish what was started so long ago.

You, the reader, hold the result in your hands. What you also hold are the prayers of all those involved with the message, those in the body and those who are not. It is our prayer that the words in this book may assist you on your journey. We pray that you find within these pages a greater appreciation for life, and a greater understanding as to your own *True Self*. Peace be with you.

# To the Readers of this Simple Message

▼

Read this book at your own pace. Some of you will read it quickly. Some, however, will take their time. Some may even put the book aside, and then pick it up again later in life. Others may get only so far and never finish. So be it.

There is no proper way to read this book. You will find your own method and pace. Our only advice is that you do not spend too much time memorizing the words on the pages. Do not expend much effort trying to intellectually grasp the concepts within. Do not take time underlining favorite sentences or writing comments in the margin.

This simple message is for your soul. It is given to encourage, to strengthen and to enhance your understanding of reality. It is a gift to enlighten the mind and enrich the heart. Therefore, do not fret if certain concepts seem beyond your intellectual understanding. There is a deeper part of your consciousness that will respond to the message.

Therefore, allow yourself to experience the words. Let the sentences enter your very being and wash over you. Intellectual understanding is of little importance. There is no test at the end of this book.

It is not enough to just read the words. Instead, allow yourself to experience the message. Realize there are forces in the universe helping you at this very moment to come to a better understanding.

To understand something, in order to truly know, it is not enough to study it. You must embrace it.

Spend time living the message. Then you will know.

# Chapter 1

## The Next Step

Life on this planet, this place called earth, this spinning sphere of joy and sorrow, of love and violence, of light and dark, is but a reflection of a greater reality. There is more to life than what you have been led to believe. There is more to be discovered, more to be experienced; so much more.

Every now and then a soul, your soul at this moment, yearns for a greater experience of life. It seeks to evolve beyond physical limitations, beyond the confines of time and space. The yearning soul seeks to know. In its restless struggle to understand, it entreats the mind to look deeper, to search for the mysterious, to find that which is hidden.

It is the power of the soul that guides the body along the path of discovery. At times it will find disappointment. Other times, there is a turn in the road and encouragement is found. The soul will continue to seek that which endures for all time, that which remains eternal while all else vanishes into the shadows of history. This life on earth, your life on this planet, is but a journey of the soul.

Every now and then a courageous soul begins to take the next step in human evolution. It is by the efforts of each individual soul yearning for awareness that human consciousness will evolve. Such an effort may seem a mere pebble thrown into the ocean; still it will have its effect.

Evolution takes time. It is a slow, often painful process of experimentation. The same force which brought the earth into existence continues its patient, subtle influence upon humanity, all the while urging it forward into a new awareness, urging it to grow and achieve a greater understanding as to its own true nature.

Creation does not stand still. On this earth, this living planet, oceans become deserts, mountains rise and fall, and the ground expands and quakes. The history of earth is a record of continual change as physical form experimented with numerous possibilities. Through the time when fish dominated as a life form, then the age of reptile, and the era of the bird, followed by the dominance of mammals, evolution allowed each distinct species to develop its potential. This is currently the age of humanity. Mankind in ascendant abides upon this earth to experiment, to discover, to evolve, to test its powers while it struggles in ignorance but grows in wisdom, learning from its mistakes and its accomplishments.

Humanity has already come to realize its physical potential, and has increased its mental abilities far beyond its original capabilities. Human potential has grown to its present state through severe tests of endurance. Human expression has developed into a vast and intricate diversity of art and music. The human need to understand led to discoveries that were once inconceivable to the human mind as it explored the realm of science and surged forward in technical advancement. All these achievements are part of the great experimentation of human evolution. And yet, for all this, mankind is still limited.

The next step is the development of humanities spiritual potential, the realization of mankind not only as a physical entity, but also as spiritual force in the universe. The next step in evolution is the development of human awareness beyond physical existence, an awareness that includes the spiritual abilities of mankind in forming its reality. This ability to expand consciousness beyond the earthly realm has always been an inherent part of human existence and the inheritance of each individual soul.

Throughout the age of man souls have emerged nudging humanity towards new discoveries, greater understandings and inevitable evolution. They spoke in the language of their culture according to the beliefs and awareness of their particular period in time. A few spoke in the language of eternity transcending era and locale; words that served as a permanent reminder of the soul's true nature.

Some of these teachers have been proclaimed saints, mystics, and prophets. Most others have remained nameless, living their earthly existence in quiet pursuit of wisdom, teaching by example and sometimes inspiring companions to take the next step. Of course, there have been others. Throughout time there have also been misguided souls who, out of ignorance or deliberate larceny, spread confusion; such souls created unnecessary obstacles with their egocentric teachings. Nevertheless, even these experiences have value as growing pains of experimentation. All experiences can offer powerful lessons.

The earth is a classroom for the soul and mistakes will be made. Much can be discovered through trial and error. Those who fear to experiment limit their education. Those who look for easy answers will be disappointed. Evolution is a slow process. It is nothing less than the exploration of human potential beyond its present limitations. Taking the next step is to discover your soul's own true nature and its spiritual capabilities. It is the internal journey that leads towards eternal life.

The journey begins by looking inward. Understand who you are and you will understand a portion of the world. Understanding a small portion of the world will lead to understanding a small part of the universe. If you can understand that small part of the universe you will glimpse a small fraction of God. To glimpse even a small fraction of God will bring understanding of your own true nature~.

Your evolution has already begun. Your soul urges you to seek answers to life's mysteries. It shall not be disappointed. If your desire is strong enough, if you are determined to overcome obstacles, if your heart's yearnings are greater than the fears of the mind, then the path of spiritual evolution will unfold.

Evolution can be painful. You will face conflict within yourself and conflict with the rest of the world. It may seem a lonely endeavor as you look within, but there are spiritual forces helping you. You have never been alone. Even at this moment as you read these words forces gather to assist, to comfort, to encourage and to protect. Have no fear. Your soul is strong. It has great power and resilience. It is eternal.

The soul has come into this world to learn, to increase its spiritual powers, and to participate in the evolution of mankind. Much of what you will accomplish will seem hidden to the rest of the world. Quiet, inner transformation is a form of personal growth that few will perceive. But, you do not take this path to achieve personal recognition. You take the next step for the sake of your soul. You seek to enlighten the mind, and to empower the heart. You evolve so the divine light that is your true nature can shine more brightly and cast away the darkness of ignorance and hopelessness.

The ability to achieve spiritual awareness is your inheritance. You claim it when you are ready to accept its responsibilities. Each individual soul, therefore, has its own set time of evolution, its own moment of awakening. A soul cannot be forced to evolve or pressured to begin its spiritual awareness. Willingness is the beginning of transformation. The decision to take the next step comes from within the soul, guided by wisdom as to when the time is right.

Certainly there are circumstances that will guide the soul towards taking the next step. Often these experiences are traumatic. Many a saint began the quest for God from the depths of despair and sorrow. Not finding comfort in the world the troubled soul searched elsewhere, thereby, taking the next step. Other souls are prompted by an intense spiritual experience such as a psychic episode, a sudden overwhelming sense of grace, or a vision of reality beyond the definitions of the world. Each soul has its own timetable, its own method of awakening for there are many paths to the top of the mountain and each journey is according to each individual's capability.

Whatever road led you to this moment, by whatever means this book has come into your hands, know that you were guided by a wisdom which surrounds you and flows through you, a wisdom which has always been with you. There is also a great strength that guides you past any obstacles that may hinder your progress. This strength is yours for the asking. Most of all, there is a love that exists. It is a love beyond your imagination, a love so real, a love so vital, that to touch upon it even lightly will change your life forever. These things and others you will come to know as you take the next step in your personal evolution. These things exist for you.

But, it is your own desire that will lead the way. It is the yearning of your soul that will start the journey. Listen to the call of your soul. Heed the inner voice that calls you to a greater awareness of reality. Step forward and come to know your *True Self*. Take the next step.

# Chapter 2

## The Ego

In the beginning, mankind was created by God as an expression of God's creativity. Because mankind was made "in the image of God," there is within you a power that is similar to the power of God. That power is creativity. Therefore, you are both a created being, as well as, a creative being, a force within the universe with the godlike ability to form your own world.

In the infancy stage of humanity, the place you call earth was quite nebular, not as dense as its present form and much smaller. In time earth grew as it gathered different energies into its gravitational field. These energies merged, were transmuted and matter came into existence. This is putting it simply, but the interaction of energies developed into all physical matter throughout the universe. What brought it all into existence is a force that can only be described as "God's creativity."

As the earth began its formation, mankind remained an infant in the womb of God. This infant, which would eventually develop into human consciousness, was born from God's creativity and emerged as a distinct manifestation of energy. With its own elemental properties, this energy came into being and began using its creative abilities to form its world. This information is being given so you may understand that human consciousness existed prior to evolving into a physical creature.

It does not matter if you understand this information, or even if you agree with it, but you are being asked to change your understanding as to the nature of physical existence. You are asked to contemplate that mankind is an evolving entity with a great capacity to learn, to grow, and to change.

With the evolution of humanity into a physical form, mankind began to perceive itself as an independent creature. Along with physical form and the illusion of independence, the ego developed as a means to aid in the survival of the species. The ego grew stronger and became the dominant thought form of mankind as attention shifted from God, the original source of creativity. Mankind's awareness separated from the realm of spirit and focused exclusively on the physical world it created. With this shift in perception, humanity separated the physical realm from spiritual reality. This only increased the illusion of being separate from God and as this limited perception increased, alienation also increased.

Eventually, mankind, feeling alone and separate from the source of all creation, also became a foreigner to its own created world. Earth became a place of fear. Survival of the physical self became humanity's sole concern. As the fear for survival increased, so did the ego. As the awareness of being God-connected diminished, the ego began to grow as humanity channeled its energy towards the preservation of the physical self. The ego became a form of self-protection, a protection against mankind's fears.

The power of the ego increased as mankind struggled to protect the physical body and supply its needs—how it was to be fed, how to clothe it, and keep it warm in winter, how to shelter it from storms, how to protect it from the threats that prowled day and night. Therefore, the way of the ego is the quest for food, clothing, habitation, and procreation to ensure continuation of the species. All of mankind's struggles, all of its achievements and all its conflicts are a result of the ego's quest for survival.

Yet, the ego is a distortion of true reality. It is a primitive form of true creative energy. With its emphasis on the physical world, the ego limits humanity's perception of reality. It sees existence only within the time between birth and death of the physical form. Spiritual reality is a mystery to the ego. After all, it is concerned only with survival on earth. That is its purpose. Spiritual concerns are beyond the abilities of the ego. While the ego remains in power mankind's capabilities of developing such spiritual attributes such as patience, wisdom and fulfilling love, are lessened by the distorted perception of the primitive ego.

For example, rather than seeking wisdom, the ego developed an intellect restricted to physical observances. Mankind's intellect evolved as a way to process and understand the experiences of physical reality. This intellect grew by cultivating a memory far greater than any other creature on earth. This development helped to insure mankind's survival. Still, it is limited. It can only process information that has a correlation in physical reality.

The human mind is capable of so much more. Some individuals have extended their abilities beyond intellectual limitations by increasing their intuitive and psychic abilities. Since these abilities challenge the ego's comprehension of reality, they are often dismissed. The intellect of the ego trusts only what it can touch, see, taste, or hear. All information must have a basis in physical reality in order to be acceptable. Anything outside the confines of ego perception is rejected as being "unrealistic."

The ego fears anything outside the realm of physical reality, anything which cannot be perceived by the senses. Again, it must be understood that the ego was developed to face the challenges of moment-to-moment survival. Therefore, it does not conceive the spiritual quality of patience as a practical virtue. Patience cannot be seen or touched or eaten. Instead, the ego knows the instant gratification of a full stomach. Having to wait for food may mean starvation, and so, the ego cannot afford to be patient.

It knows the immediate need for clothing and shelter, whereas, waiting too long may mean death from exposure. To the ego this is reality. As far as the body is concerned these things are true. However, the fault of the ego lies in its imposing its need for immediate results on all aspects of life. True patience comes from the understanding that life is eternal that the soul's journey continues beyond space and time.

Then there is love. Much more information will be given on this subject later in the book. For now, in this moment, try to understand that the ego has created a lesser form of love, which is a distortion of the great power of spiritual love. For some people love is an obscure concept, an elusive feeling sometimes glimpsed but never attained. For others, love is a temporary sensation dependent on outside forces, such as, another individual, a place, a pet, and for some, a career. The ego has limited love by objectifying it and thereby making it a precious commodity.

Keep in mind that the ego serves as a means of self-protection. Love makes it feel too vulnerable. Though the ego seeks love it will still keep its distance from the experience of knowing true love. Only when the ego has determined all circumstances to be safe and secure, that the right person has been found, that the pet will not bite, that the career has its rewards, then it will allow an inkling of love to be experienced. Even then it will keep self-preservation as a priority.

Until the next step in evolution is taken, until the ego is regulated to its proper and lesser place in human awareness, it will dominate human action on earth. True protection of the body can be achieved by increasing intuitive awareness, that is, sensing physical danger before it happens. The well being of the physical body will increase with a balance of physical energies harmonizing with spiritual forces.

These concepts are introduced so you may begin to understand that what you call physical reality and spiritual reality are not two separate and distinct realms of existence. Though there are differences in vibration, nevertheless, they come from the same source. All energies come from God's creativity. These forces work together within you. You are a physical entity at this time, but you are also a spiritual being. It is only the ego that creates a distinction between the two. It is the limited understanding of the ego that causes an imbalance by focusing on the fears of human existence. The ego cannot conceive of spiritual forces which are unseen by the human eye. According to the ego's criteria, these spiritual forces cannot exist. Only the ego can protect the body, so it would have you believe.

To protect itself, the ego creates the ideal of a "perfect body." Throughout time, and according to specific cultural attitudes, this ideal body may change form, but it always emphasizes how well the body can insure survival. The ego distorts the true beauty of the physical body by its standards of sexual attraction, muscular prowess, youth, and physical health. By settling for superficial appearances, blind to the true beauty of the body—wonderful creation that it is—the ego limits the body's potential.

To dissect the physical body down to bones, blood and muscle is to see only a small part of its purpose. The body you have is a world unto its own. It is a creative expression in which the soul has come to learn, to grow, to experiment and to increase its spiritual abilities. The physical sensations of the body serve as a classroom for the soul. It conveys information on a feeling level. In turn, the physical body also serves as a conduit, which can harness specific energies found throughout the universe, and channels them into the physical realm. Many who are called to be healers on earth learn to use energy to correct imbalances in the body. As mankind begins the next step in evolution more healers will appear.

Many of these healers, however, will be more concerned with spiritual well being than with the health of the body. Regardless of any illness, regardless of any perceived flaws or what you would call a handicap, the body is a marvelous vehicle. Whatever its condition the body will serve its purpose, and then be returned to the earth while the soul continues its journey.

The human mind may understand this, but the ego with its sole concern to protect the body will continue to identify with the physical form. To the ego, spiritual reality either doesn't exist or is a vague concept.

Because it came into being in order to help the body survive, the ego separates itself not only from the spiritual realm, but from other physical forms as well. With separation, there is loneliness. With feeling alone there is vulnerability. Everything becomes a challenge. Threats are ever present and life becomes something to be conquered. Awareness is limited to the needs of the self above all else. Harmony is forgotten. Virtue loses its importance. Spirituality becomes clouded and God becomes distant and uncaring.

As the ego perceived the earth to be threatening, spirituality, which cannot be seen with the human eye, became even more frightening. Even God became vengeful. For many people the spiritual realm became something to be appeased, or controlled. For too many people it became something to be ignored and forgotten.

And yet, the seeds of mankind's potential remain. Within your legends, your myths, your various religions with their stories of Gardens of Eden, and within the tales of ancient advanced civilizations is the collective memory of a time when humanity was not separate. They recall a time when human consciousness was one with God, connected to earth and to all of creation. These stories recall the time when humanity truly used its creative abilities. Such stories serve as reminders. A time will come again, when individuals will take the next step in evolution, creatively expanding their awareness beyond the illusion of separation to achieve a greater union of spiritual and earthly forces.

Until then the world remains at the present stage of ego. The "original sin," as it is called, is simply the emergence of the ego. The "fall from grace," is only an illusion of separation. Adam and Eve were never tossed out of the beautiful paradise of God's creation. They walked out. By eating the fruit of the tree of knowledge, they suddenly became aware of their differences. For the first time they realized they were naked and they felt ashamed. "And Adam and Eve hid themselves from the Lord God," so it is written.

Spiritual unity was broken. Paradise was lost. Shame, sorrow and fear became a part of human existence. As they were told, "your eyes will be opened and ye shall be as gods, knowing good and evil." And so, it came to pass. With such knowledge, Adam and Eve left the garden. It was not banishment. It was not God's judgment, as some would claim. God did not separate from humanity. Just as a child has the blood of its parents, the creative force that is God remains within you.

And, just as a baby grows into a child and learns to walk, so did humanity have to discover its own true power and full potential. Mankind had to take responsibility for its own participation in the creative process. As an infant still close to the God Force, mankind's creativity came easily. So much so, that consciousness at that time was unaware of how much it was actively creating the world. Being unaware, human consciousness did not take responsibility and mistakes were made. Even at this present time, the people of earth still refuse to acknowledge their own participation in creating the world. The ego is concerned only with present time and does not consider the individual's partnership in the continual process of evolution; a partnership that existed in the past is involved with the present and continues into the future.

There exists on earth remnants of the earlier stages of human creativity, not many, but some still exist. Scientists and archaeologists will not understand fully what they have found since these objects do not conform to the current perspective of history. These ancient artifacts are testimony to previous ways of existence on earth. They are the results of earlier experiments in human creativity.

It was during that stage of experimentation, mankind, like a young child, first became aware of its own creative abilities. At the same time a distortion in human thought came into being as well. Mankind began to think of itself as an independent creative source. Mankind believed it was the center of the universe.

The memory of this stage in evolution is recalled in the story of God's beloved angel who defied Divine authority, thinking itself to be greater than God. The independent nature of Lucifer, or Satan, who tried to be as God, was separated from God and cast to earth. This story remains wonderful symbolism for the selfish nature of the ego creating a world of darkness, blind to its own divine nature as a beloved of God.

The battle against evil is human consciousness struggling to see beyond the darkness of limited perception. It is the battle to overcome blindness and ignorance. The journey to God is the flight of the soul returning to the center of all creation. The next step in this journey is to overcome the limitations of the ego, to expand awareness beyond mere physical existence, and increase the spiritual powers of the soul on earth.

The ego itself is not evil. It is not a sin. There are no real sins, only ignorance. The horror and pain of the world is created out of ignorance and the ego's blindness. Remember, the ego is only a primitive way of being which has come to dominate human awareness. It will not always be this way.

Humanity has begun to enter a new age and is currently experiencing the growing pains of evolution. By facing these challenges that occur during times of transition, individuals will come to discover the true power of spirit working in their lives. They will come to acknowledge their own responsibility in the process of human evolution. People will begin to learn there are alternatives to egotistical thinking.

For now it is enough to understand the limitations of the ego. Neither judge the ego nor cherish it. Simply acknowledge it as one aspect of human development. It is, however, not the only one. Since the ego was formed in the beginning of mankind's appearance on earth, it remains primitive. The vibrations of egotistical thought patterns remain close to physical body because its function is to protect the body.

The energy field of the ego encompasses the body like a shield. Therefore, it has a low frequency and its creative ability is limited and of temporary endurance.

You have experienced this energy shield on many occasions. For instance, the energy field of the ego will resonate with another's ego when there is a shared vibration such as mutual intellectual interest, sexual attraction, and especially when there is animosity. During a situation when two ego are in conflict the force of the ego's energy becomes stronger, more protective, and if provoked, antagonistic.

Opposite that, in a situation where there is love, or a spiritual connection between two souls, the shields will be momentarily lowered. A higher vibration of love is exchanged. This sudden experience of love is so often described as euphoria as the influx of this unique vibration infuses the individual on both a physical and spiritual level. In those moments an individual can experience existence without the ego, which is why many people claim to feel so vulnerable when in love.

And yet, should the individual in love feel offended or threatened in any way, the ego shield of self-protection comes back into place. Because the ego has grown so powerful in human consciousness, feelings of separation, of fear, of anger, and confusion return all too quickly. The beautiful feeling of love abates. Loneliness, which is a profound sensation of separation, can persist even in a relationship with another soul. It is the shield of the ego causing that separation.

When feelings of separation become overwhelming, people begin searching for a cure. They search for a new way of being through therapies, religions, various cults and social organizations, books and academic instruction. There is much to be gained by this, but be forewarned. The current egotistical perspective of the world will influence much of the information found. In many cases the ego will be reinforced rather than diminished.

When you desire to seek out who you truly are, who God intended you to be, then begin to seek a new way of walking on this earth. When you yearn to discover the potential of your soul, then seek to change your thinking. Realize there can be a different way to travel in the world, a different way to relate to the people in your life, and even a new way to see yourself. When the desire becomes strong enough, you will begin to discover other ways do exist.

# Chapter 3

## Begin the Journey

Find a quiet time, a time when you know there will be nothing to disturb you. Make the time, if you have to. Don't wait for it to be given to you. You are going to take a short journey. If for some reason you cannot take this journey physically, you can do it in your mind by visualizing each step.

Begin by sitting at home; wherever you call home, in a room you are most comfortable. Take a few deep breaths and relax. So much time, so much effort is given to the demands of the ego. So much energy is given to day-to-day struggles. For this moment let it go. For this brief time listen to your heart. Give yourself this gift of time, a gift for your soul. Relax and turn your attention inward.

Before the journey can begin prepare yourself by considering this message: you have not sinned against God. You have not fallen from grace. You have made no mistakes that can sever your connection to the origin of all creativity, the source of all power, the fountain of all love. You are in ego, a stage of development, and you will grow beyond its limitations.

All you experience in life is but a step in evolution. If there is poverty in your life, realize it is only a stage. You may have material abundance, but that too, is only a transient state of existence. The feelings of loneliness, the feelings of separation, all your doubts and all your fears, are simply a small part of your life. Though you may hold onto self-confidence, though you cling to those experiences, which please the ego and give you satisfaction, take a moment to understand they cannot last. Everything changes.

There is more to life, more to be discovered. Realize that much more awaits you. These discoveries will come to you when you desire such knowledge. It will come when you are willing to sacrifice the ego and its limitations. If you desire to have true understanding, true love and acceptance, then you must let go of the ego.

Before you begin this short journey take a moment to call upon the spiritual forces of the universe. No matter what stage in life you are presently in, call upon God and the force of God's love to come into your life. There is no penance to be done. There is no confession of past sins to be made. You have made mistakes in the past. You will make mistakes in the future. Learn from those experiences, make the necessary changes, and then continue.

Do not be discouraged by anything you would call a failure. Discouragement is a trick of the ego that seeks immediate results. It is the ego insisting on a perfection that does not exist. Leave perfection to God. Find your perfection through God.

By asking the spiritual forces of God for help you step beyond the ego. You reach beyond your own limitations to that which is greater. You acknowledge spiritual reality as a vital power. You must simply ask with a humble heart and with great courage for God to come into your life.

Do it now. Do it this very moment, even if you are doubtful, even if it feels awkward. Close your eyes, relax, then simply say, "Be with me."

When you are ready open your eyes and turn your attention outward. Look around you. Look at the floor. Look at the walls. Look at the furniture in the room. Look at all that surrounds you, but do not judge any of it. Do not notice that one thing is beautiful and another thing is old and ugly. Resist the temptation to change what you see. Simply look at it for what it is. Realize you have created everything in that room. It is quite simple. Through your own desire and effort you have brought these objects into your life.

Now go out into the world. Go where people have established residences and businesses, wherever there is a village or town or city. Go for a walk. We will be with you. Walk down streets without a destination. Just walk and observe. Look around the neighborhoods. Look at the buildings and cars. Observe the people passing by. Glance at the sky and the ground beneath your feet. Again, there is no judgment. Just look as if standing at a distance. Take it all in; the sights, the sounds, the smells of what mankind has created. As you watch consider your part in creating all this. All you see was brought into the world for a purpose and you have taken an active part in its creation. You may not understand the purpose of all you see, but realize by being on earth you are responsible for its existence.

Continue to walk. Continue to look. As you do bring into mind all people who are a part of your life. Think about all relationships you experience—with family, with friends, with those who share your bed, with coworkers and employers. Consider that you brought them into your life for a purpose no matter how long the relationship may last, no matter how long or how short you may know these people. You are as responsible for the relationship as they are. You are in their life for a purpose.

There is no need to ask why at this point in the journey. Do not wonder at this time what the purpose may be and do not judge any of the relationships as either good or bad. As you walk simply allow their faces to appear in your mind. Acknowledge them and realize it was your power that has brought them to you, and it is their power that brought you into their lives. It may be difficult, but do not judge them. Quietly watch their faces appear before you. If you find yourself dwelling on a particular person either through love or anger, then actively divert your attention towards something else. It takes time and effort learning to look at people and events with equanimity. You will learn to view such things without the limited judgments of the ego.

When you feel ready to do so, return home. On your return bring together all you have seen. Extend your awareness beyond your immediate surroundings and visualize the entire world. Let whatever images, whatever beliefs you have about the world come forth. Images of poverty may come to mind, but consider as well the abundance. Visions of war may be seen, but contemplate visions of peace. You may be aware of conflict between individuals and between nations, but realize there are those who bring love into the world as well. Consider all these things and realize you have a part in creation. Realize you can choose what you wish to bring into the world.

Once you have returned to your home avoid rushing back into your daily routine. Do not think you have to make up for lost time, as the ego would have you believe. To the ego anything which does not have to do with the physical body is a waste of time and, therefore, impractical. If you believe inner development and spiritual growth is not worth some time and effort, then put away this book. You are too willing to settle for less.

If you returned home pleased and satisfied with everything you have observed, you should put this book down. You have grown too comfortable with the ways of the world. You do not have the desire to grow beyond the limited image you have of yourself and the world around you. Put the book away. Your time has not yet come.

If, instead, you realized how much of the world is a reflection of mankind's ego, if you realized how much has been created out of fear and separation, you can also realize it does not have to remain that way.

If you can look around you and say, "it is not enough, there must be more to life," then continue to read. Begin to discover within yourself the power to create. Begin to allow your *True Self* to be revealed. Begin to manifest your spiritual abilities in the world. Desire these things to be your reality and you will begin to experience those aspects of God's love working through you at this very moment. Shifts in your consciousness, in your physical energy, and in your relationship with the world have already begun.

You take this journey towards greater awareness, not because you fear the world, or because you have judged one thing or another as bad. You take this journey because within you is that spark of life that will not settle for less. Continue your journey and grow. Know it is possible. Know it can begin now.

CHAPTER 4

▼

# BEYOND THE EGO

Beyond the image you see in the mirror, beyond whatever thoughts you have of yourself, beyond everything that has been taught and everything which has been imposed upon you, there is a part of you which is eternal, a part of you which is connected to the source of all creation, a part which guides each step taken on earth. Beyond all thoughts as to who you are or who you should be in life, there exists your "*True Personality.*

Who you are, who you have always been, is God's expression of creativity. You are a wonderful, beautiful masterpiece created by a great artist. You are of brilliant color and wondrous form. You have been created with love, care, and great wisdom. All these things are found within your *True Personality.*

It is the greater element of your being, the very essence of life dwelling within you. The *True Personality* does not seek a reason to exist. It knows existence is its own reward.

It does not ask the reason for being born. The *True Personality* knows that to be born into this world is to partake in life and embrace all it has to offer. The *True Personality*, with courage and wisdom, faces all aspects of life: trials and tribulations, victories and growth, birth and death. The *True Personality* comes upon this earth knowing what sorrows and pains are to be faced, what joy and love it will encounter, what lessons are valuable. It knows life on earth to be a worthwhile opportunity for advancement, a chance to gather knowledge, a way to increase its skills and to enhance its ability to love.

This *True Personality*, the fire of life that has given you human form, is the reason why you wake each morning. It is why you take a breath without having to think about it. It is why you continue to struggle against obstacles, against thoughts that would make you weary, make you feel defeated.

The *True Personality* is a powerful force. It has always been with you. It is always within you. It has been the guiding power in your life before you came upon this earth. It is the eternal force that continues once you move beyond the earthly realm.

You have come into the physical body in order to experience, to learn, to create, and to be an expression of God's love. Your *True Personality* knows this. It has great wisdom, great love, and great joy. We say again, it is the essence of life, the creative spark of divine creativity within you. It is your *True Personality* that is united to God and all of God's creation.

Few people come to know this spark of light. Few even acknowledge it exists. The ego has shadowed its beauty. The wonderful colors that make up your *True Self* became darkened by fears and doubts. The beautiful masterpiece cannot be seen because the ego denies it, seeing only the needs of the physical body as important. Even to those who have sought this magnificent beauty, it remained a hidden mystery because they did not look within themselves.

The *True Personality*, your *True Self*, may seem lost to you. It can never be lost. You have limited the power of the *True Personality* by limiting the way you see yourself. The limitations of the ego formed an identity solely on its experiences on earth and became forgetful of its spiritual power and true divine nature. By forming a temporary personality dominated by the ego you restricted your experiences on earth to the mere physical aspects of existence. It is not the ego, but the *True Personality* that guides you into the realm of earthly experience. It does so with wisdom, knowing what circumstances on earth will lead to greater understandings. The *True Personality* knows it will come upon the earth and develop an ego personality that will follow a certain course of action leading to the lessons it seeks. It does so in order to gather knowledge.

This temporary personality begins its formation prior to physical birth. The emotions, thoughts and situation of the parents help form the emerging personality. A fetus registers subtle and minute impressions ranging from shifts in the mother's body chemistry to the emotional atmosphere outside the womb. The emerging personality begins gathering information immediately, fully aware of the challenges and risks of physical birth, and there are many. After all, it is far more difficult to come into the world than it is to leave.

A soul with a strong *True Personality* will determine the wisest time and situation to enter the world. Should the soul deem circumstances to be unfavorable it will refuse to participate in the formation of the fetus and a miscarriage will result. There are some souls, however, so anxious to return to earth, they will accept any opportunity regardless of situation and time. The consequences of such births are varied. Some complete the transition into the material world, others may be born premature, and others have only a short duration of physical life. It was simply not their time to appear on earth.

The wise soul enters the earthly realm knowing the lessons it will encounter. It chooses the circumstances that will lead to desired experiences from which it will gain new knowledge. The soul begins immediately with the conception of the physical body. Every heartbeat is felt; every shift in temperature is remembered as the fetus takes shape. The soul and other spiritual forces, spirit guides as they are often called, will exert an influence on the physical formation of the fetus. If a spiritual lesson is to be experienced by inhabiting a less than perfect body, then the soul will help alter its development and form the vehicle best suited to its needs. It is only the ego that insists on a "perfect" body, seeing anything less as a tragedy.

After its passage through the womb, the infant soul lingers in the spiritual realm as it slowly becomes aware of physical reality. This is a time of transition. This period of innocence, of quiet purity, is a stage in which the individual soul begins to forget the spiritual realm and prepares itself for a new adventure. As the infant's awareness of the physical world increases, ego-consciousness develops. With growing awareness, there is a greater demand on the infant to focus outward into the material world and spiritual consciousness decreases.

Eventually the infant becomes cognizant of its surroundings, becomes more aware of physical reality. The infant becomes increasingly sensitive to the energies within its environment. The initial and strongest impressions are drawn from the immediate family atmosphere. These first impressions form the foundation of how the personality will view the world, how it will react in the world, and how it sees itself in the world.

This ego personality is then further developed according to the specific time, placement, and external influences on the soul during its beginning years on earth. Time has its importance as each period of human history offers a unique perspective. Where the infant is born will determine cultural and religious attributes. External influences ranging from childhood disease to the interaction of parents and siblings will determine future reactions of the temporary personality during its journey in the world.

Therefore, your strengths and weakness, your likes and dislikes, are adaptations formed by the ego according to its experiences since birth. Your thoughts and opinions are the ego's reactions to external stimuli. What you think of yourself and of others, how you see life and the world around you are limited to what you have been exposed to on earth. But do not believe the ego personality is all you are or all you have been. This life you live is one of many.

There is, as well, remnant memories of previous lives on earth, for you have been a participant throughout human evolution, living many lives, having many delightful existences, each one adding to knowledge, each one guided by your *True Personality*. With each new journey on earth, with every new existence as a human, the old ego personalities fade from awareness. Yet the knowledge gained by those past experiences remain with the *True Self.* Just as the personality of a child ceases to exist with maturity, the memories of childhood remain. So it is with each new life upon the earth; previous lives may be forgotten with each new manifestation on earth, but memories are retained.

New circumstances form a new personality, but remnant memories of other lives linger and often influence your present life. Unexplained fears and ambitions, particular likes and dislikes, haunting compulsions; many aspects of the ego personality retain recollections of previous existences. Fear of water may speak of a previous life that ended in drowning. Overeating may be a reaction to having once starved to death. A particular talent may have first been developed in another lifetime. Even relationships are often a continuation of involvement with someone known from another existence.

Life on earth has much to offer and one life is not enough. The varieties of experiences are plentiful, offering many opportunities for those souls desiring further knowledge. Each life is an experiment. Each life is a new chance. Each life is step in the journey of evolution. It is important to acknowledge the continuation of life through many existences in order to understand that your current personality, who you think you are at this moment, is a temporary state of existence. Your current personality, which you hold so dear, is the result of your limited experiences on earth. Those experiences are limited because they exclude the spiritual nature of reality, as we have said, by focusing so intently on the physical realm.

Because the ego has been formed by external stimulus, it will continue to define itself, even attempt to change itself, through external opportunities. For instance, the ego will seek fulfillment through social organizations, religious structures and political affiliations. By its allegiance with certain segments of society or cultures, by identifying with professional careers or sexual orientation, the ego defines its sense of self within strict self-imposed boundaries.

Each time you have told yourself, "I am this," or "I am that," you kept yourself limited. You have conformed to a particular way of thinking and a particular way of acting in the world. You have restricted yourself to a certain code of behavior, dictated not by true desire of the heart, but by outside influences. You have allowed external impressions to determine your identity, rather than allowing the spiritual force of your *True Self* to emerge.

All this is a result of the ego looking outside the self for a personal sense of identity, for a sense of belonging, for a reason to live. Whenever that ego-defined reason for existence begins to disintegrate, to show flaws and fade away, depression occurs. When the ego's concepts of self-identity cease to exist, such as the loss of a business, the loss of a lover, or an injury to the body, confusion and depression may result. Those are the times when you are forced to question the validity of your own identity. For instance, when a political party suddenly shows itself to be less than honorable, or when a religious organization suddenly appears less holy than its public image; this affects how you see yourself. Suddenly you are not as honorable as you thought, you are not as holy as you believed. When you lose a job, suddenly you are not as valuable as you assumed.

When the ego's limited sense of identity is threatened in any manner, you experience feelings of loss, abandonment, outrage and despair. You lose your sense of place in the world. Your preconceived purpose in life becomes meaningless. Feelings of despair, confusion and outrage are the ego's fear of losing its identity. The ego is fearful because losing its identity is experienced as losing the ability to survive. The ego fears its death.

Experience the depression. It is a time of mourning as the old self fades and the *True Self* begins to emerge. Though the cloud of depression may blind you, eventually it will pass. Your *True Personality* will strengthen you in times of sorrow and loss. When it does pass do not go seeking outside yourself once again. Do not seek resurrection by reconstructing what you once possessed. Look, instead, within your own being, your own heart and soul, to discover your *True Self*. You will find it when you refuse to limit yourself.

When you claim, "I am a man."

"I am a woman."

"I am a Democrat."

"I am a Socialist."

"I am a heterosexual."

"I am a homosexual."

"I am a poet, an artist or a prisoner," then you have limited yourself.

By these and other definitions you've adopted a role in life and made it your reason for living. It is the ego's quest for personal power, its way of surviving the challenges on earth. It is how the ego justifies its existence. Great effort is taken to maintain, protect and defend that image. Any threat to that identity, real or imagined, becomes a threat to survival.

You then surround yourself with others who fit within these categories and a group consciousness is formed. This consciousness is the result of the collective ego forming a safe and familiar environment whose participants agree to unspoken rules of thought and action. Your sense of self, the range of your thoughts and actions, are then limited to the standards of a collective ego.

Though this may be an individual's attempt to discover more about its own personality, an attempt to grow into a new sense of self, it is still driven by the ego seeking outside validation. Because the ego is threatened by the illusion of separation, an individual will seek to enhance his or her identity by joining a particular group, uniting with other individuals who also feel separate. Together, however, they are no longer alone. United by shared interests and a mutual outlook on life, an organization is formed to empower the ego. All groups become organizations. All groups gather and form a collective ego.

Informal organizations include family relationships, groups of friends, racial and cultural preferences. Formal organizations include religious, political, business, or social structures. Yet all groups, no matter how they are formed, maintain a similar purpose. Each gives the ego a sense of self, a sense of protection, and an image of being unique.

Unless an organization can present itself as being unique, with the ability to meet the ego's needs better than any other organization, it will cease to exist. The collective ego of an organization must claim to offer its participants something that cannot be found elsewhere. It must offer the individual ego an identity greater than what other organizations offer.

This is known as the "herding instinct" of ego consciousness. It expresses itself in the thought "there is safety in numbers." Safety from what? Safety from those who are not part of the herd, those other organizations, those outside the family, those of another religion, race, or culture. By becoming part of a collective ego, the individual seeks protection from the self-created illusion of danger. United with others who share a similar outlook on life, the individual ego feels stronger. This strength comes from compatible egos encouraging a mutual perception of reality. In order to be compatible the individual ego must conform to the doctrines of the organization.

To insure conformity of thought and action, every organization, formal and informal, must distinguish itself from other groups. The stricter the organization, the more dogmatic its outlook, the greater the difference between "us" and "them." The collective ego uses the illusion of separation to justify its existence. Those outside the organization are not to be trusted. They are inferior. They are sinful. They are a threat because they are not one of us. Without this conflict the collective ego has no purpose.

Opposition strengthens the collective identity of an organization. A religious institution, therefore, sees a different religion with a different name for God as a threat. A particular political viewpoint must vanquish another. In business there must be competition. Anyone outside the family is less valuable than a blood relation. Those who dress differently are dismissed as inferior. Sexual preference outside established morals is a threat to society. Those who disagree with the organization's limited perception of reality, become ostracized, driven from the family, dismissed as a renegade and isolated as a traitor.

Within an organization conformity must be tested. Competition is maintained to insure loyalty to the group. Titles are bestowed, rewards are given to the worthy, and punishments inflicted on those who falter. In religion it is the promise of salvation or the punishment of damnation. In business it is financial reward or termination. In politics it is the illusion of power or failure into obscurity. Each group becomes an extension of the family with every individual vying for attention, striving for acknowledgment, fearful of the withdrawal of love.

An individual ego, fearful of rejection and separation, will conform to prescribed patterns of conduct in seeking the safety and protection of a particular organization. Being surrounded by others who act the same, who dress the same, who are in agreement as to what is right and what is wrong, an individual begins to believe he or she is not alone. To maintain this sense of belonging, you must deny who you truly are and keep your *True Personality* hidden by suppressing any tendency to be different. You must keep your *True Self* so buried that no one may see. This is done out of fear.

Often it is this same fear of being alone which compels a person into a relationship with another individual. Again, the ego looks outside itself for a sense of identity, using another individual to supply its needs, to uphold and enhance the ego's definition of reality. On a deep, emotional level, the ego interacts with another ego to compliment its own self-image, or to supplement a lack in abilities.

This denies the validity of another's existence. Unless there is a Karmic connection from a previous life and two souls are in agreement to unite once again on earth, the ego will choose a partner based on a superficial, but personal criteria, such as, physical appearance, social abilities, material wealth, and conformity of goals and opinions; whatever meets the needs of the ego. Yet, no one comes into the world to cater to another's ego.

What often results is a conflict between two egos, each fighting to satisfy its own desires. Often the experience of love ends in disappointment when an individual comes to realize that the ego's perception of another was only an illusion; an example of the ego's inability to see beyond a narrow view of reality. The ego's focus on the superficial, and blindness to spiritual reality, contradicts the true beauty of two souls traveling together upon the earth.

Human relationships are complex, rich in meaning, tenacious and delicate. As the world is still within the stage of ego consciousness, relationships on all levels are limited in their interactions as the ego can only express a primitive vibration of love. True love knows no limitations. True love as expressed through the *True Personality* acknowledges another soul's journey, shares in another's discoveries, is enhanced by the differences in experiences and is supportive of another's struggle to learn.

There is another way to exist in the world. There is a way to rise out of the entanglements of the ego. There is a way to heal all wounds, to comfort the broken heart, to find an end to petty struggles. It lies within you. It may have been forgotten, but it still remains. It is the *True Personality*, the eternal self embraced by God, connected to all of creation. It is the Divine light of existence that can never be extinguished.

The *True Personality* knows it is more than an image in a mirror, more than the clothes that adorn the body, more than its occupation on earth. The *True Self* does not live by bread alone.

Within your *True Self* lie your unique gifts. It has within its power a greater awareness of reality, a greater sense of what it means to be alive on earth. It can see beyond the limits of time and space. It is light and life itself.

It does not know fear. It sees beyond the illusion of separation. It can never be alone. The *True Self* is a part of God and has all the spiritual forces, angelic and saintly, as its companions. The *True Personality* looks lovingly upon others who travel this earth. It sees individuals as creations of God, regardless of how they may think, regardless of how they dress, or what form and color they have chosen for a body.

The *True Self* sees the common denominator of all of creation. It sees the beauty and majesty of God's light. How can there be separation?

The *True Self* is wisdom. There dwells within it knowledge gathered from many lives and many experiences. It knows the dark and it know the light and it knows the difference. It knows without doubt that God's light will always be, and the darkness is already conquered. The increased awareness of the *True Personality* is sensitive to any challenges to its spiritual well being. From wisdom gathered from previous experiences on earth, the power of the *True Self* is aware of that which threatens its growth. It has the power to destroy illusion.

You are a spiritual being, a creation of God's love. You possess a great inheritance. The potential of the human spirit is great. You are capable of more, so much more.

You have grown from an infant into a child, from childhood you evolved into an adult, as an adult you continue to learn and grow. With each step your physical body grew and your personality changed. Life is growth. Life is change. The next step is to mature beyond the restrictions of ego and allow the *True Personality* its expression on earth.

Your sense of identity will change. The way you see reality will be altered. Relationships will take on a new meaning. You will depart from the collective consciousness, even if it means standing alone, so you may look within your own soul and see the beauty of God's creation. By the spiritual power of the *True Personality* you will create a new existence. There will still be challenges and struggles. There will still be lessons to increase knowledge. But, with a greater awareness and with newfound abilities, you will meet the demands of earthly existence with a deeper understanding, an inner strength, and a love that cannot be diminished.

The *True Personality* is God's glorious moment of creativity in which you where formed. It is the *True Personality*, bright and glorious, which will exist forever when all else has vanished. Though hidden by fear and doubt, though concealed by ambition and striving, though darkened by sorrow and pain, the *True Self* remains untainted.

Look within. Acknowledge you are an expression of God, worthy of life, generous in love, eternal in nature and creative beyond imagination. Let go of the ego and its obsessions with the body. Let your spiritual nature protect and guide you. Let your *True Personality* emerge. It is the light Jesus spoke of, the light kept hidden beneath the bushel.

Let it be revealed.

# Chapter 5

# A Simple Experiment

It is impossible for the ego to fully understand the *True Personality*. It does not want to know. *True Personality* is eternal. The ego is concerned only with the temporal. The ego searches outside itself for survival, always seeking those things the body needs. The ego is concerned with what is lacking: food, clothing, possessions, and personal power. The ego does not look within unless forced to do so and even then it is inadequate. It cannot comprehend the power of spiritual reality.

It cannot conceive of finding within itself a sense of quiet satisfaction, a sense of inner peace and inner fulfillment. The ego's purpose is to look outward, finding fulfillment through food, clothing, home, health, and personal power. But, hunger returns, clothing becomes worn, any home on earth is temporary, and the body will grow old and weary. Personal power is an illusion. And so, the quest of the ego is unending—never satisfied. It is always searching, always looking to the world for sustenance.

It seeks love through another. It finds purpose through labor. It seeks security through material wealth. It craves pleasure and joy by exciting the physical senses. In spite of all its efforts the ego knows that time will someday conquer and death of the physical body is inevitable. And so, the ego never finds peace. It faces each day as another struggle to survive. The ego has its place in human awareness, but not to the extent it has come to dominate human thinking. It is as if you exercised one part of the body while neglecting the other parts. Over time one part becomes strong while the others atrophy. The domination of the ego has submerged mankind's spiritual nature.

Begin to see yourself not just as a creature walking the earth, but a vital presence in the universe, a part of heaven, and a part of God. You are a force of creativity. You have powers and abilities waiting to be put to use. The *True Personality* is complete unto itself, knowing full well the interaction of spiritual reality and the physical realm. This the ego does not understand. It divides reality into small and narrow perceptions, seeing only separation, creating for itself a rift between the two forces. Such a separation cannot exist. While distinctions, such as male and female, sky and earth, rain and fire, sun and moon, do exist and each speaks of the variety of God's creativity, still all things come from the same source. All are one.

Your *True Personality* is aware of this. *True Personality* knows wholeness, completeness, and totality of being. It knows it is a part of creation now and forever. To discover the *True Personality* you must begin to discipline your mind. Begin to understand that all you want, everything you need, is already within you. It is all contained within your *True Self.* As a part of creation, what could possibly be lacking in your life? What is it that you are missing? What do you not already possess?

The *True Personality* knows the needs of the body and has created the ego as an aspect of physical awareness. Human evolution depended on the ego, but evolution must continue. Mankind's potential is not yet realized. The ego is insufficient, only a small part of human development which continues to display its inadequacy.

An ego-created identity is too small to contain the multi-dimensional beauty of the human spirit. Such an image only limits what is possible. People assume that their ego-created self-image is all they are; all they are capable of being. Even though they may be unhappy with themselves, thinking they are not beautiful enough, not in possession of enough money, though ambition is never satisfied, though the quest for happiness seems unending, still they are quite protective of their adopted identity. They defend the limited concept they have of themselves whenever that concept is threatened.

The ego presents itself as the key to survival and, therefore, perceives any threat to its identity as a threat to survival. When talking about the *True Personality*, when expressing its attributes and abilities, an individual may begin to feel a bit of panic. He or she will experience denial as a means of protecting the ego. For some individuals the loss of their limited self-image is felt to be a death of the self. They fear losing themselves if they step beyond the boundaries set by the ego. They cling to the ego-identity with its beliefs, opinions and fears as if it were their salvation. They do not desire to see anything that may challenge the ego's dominance.

Because the ego was created for physical survival of the species, it fears loss of any kind. Discovering your *True Self* does take sacrifice, but all you must give up is the limited concept that you have of yourself. By sacrificing the egotistical perception of reality you can begin to discover a greater self-awareness. You can begin to discover who you truly are. When you give up the limited viewpoints of the ego you can discover the many gifts waiting to be put into use.

Beyond the ego is the ability to express spiritual power into the physical world. Beyond the ego is a self-awareness of beauty, joy and love. Beyond the ego is the understanding you are a reflection of God's light, a powerful force expressed in a moment of time, expressed for all of eternity.

Your *True Self* is the fruit of God's creativity born out of love, out of joy, magnificent and beautiful, shining as a bright light for the world to see.

There is nothing to be hidden, nothing to be protected, nothing lacking in your life because you are secure in the knowledge that you are of God.

Created by God, the *True Personality* is also creative, and has manifested itself into the world in order to learn certain valuable lessons. The *True Personality* comes to earth seeking certain experiences so it may increase its knowledge, develop its abilities, and grow in awareness. Though it comes into the realm of ego—consciousness, the *True Personality* is always in a state of love, always connected by love to God.

The next step in human evolution is relinquishing the power of the ego, diminishing its dominance to its proper place, and allowing the creative power of the *True Personality* to heal the earth, transform human relationships, and begin the process of creating a new existence. That is not to say the earth will become perfect. The earth will always remain a classroom offering unique experiences particular to the physical realm. As an individual allowing the *True Self* to emerge, you will still experience pain, still know the sensations of illness, still partake of the enriching and wonderful realm of physical and emotional sensations. The expression of the *True Personality* into the world is not the goal you are trying to reach. There are no goals. Creativity is unending.

However, by allowing the *True Self* to take its place in human consciousness, you take the next step in evolution. You take a different approach towards learning the mysteries of existence on earth and throughout the universe. There will still be challenges. There will still be experimentation along with its failures and wonderful accomplishments; however, with the influence of the *True Personality* an individual will find greater creative powers, increased abilities, and a new perception as to the nature of reality.

Even with the manifestation of *True Personality* on earth, there will still remain differences between individuals, each according to their particular vibration, each according to their expertise in creativity, and each according to their specific lessons on earth. To put it simply, with mankind's next step into a greater consciousness, all individuals will share in a more coherent effort towards survival, with an increased spiritual awareness, and a willingness to accept greater responsibility for their personal and collective actions.

What changes is the motivation. *True Personality* is motivated by love. The ego is motivated by fear. Look around you. Observe the people surrounding you. All are individuals. All appear different. Yet, all are motivated by fear. All are working within the primitive stage of ego. Therefore, it is the internal motivation behind creative action that shows the greater difference between *True Personality* and the ego. To act in love, to create with spiritual awareness, and to learn with increased sensitivity are the gifts of the *True Self*.

Before this can be discovered you must first move beyond the restrictions of fear. Your ego will fight for survival and will put up defenses of denial, of confusion, and sometimes anger. You must discipline the mind and begin to accept the awareness that you are more than you have been led to believe.

You must be conscious that beyond the limitations of the ego there is more. Beyond the feelings of unworthiness, beyond the constant feelings of deficiency, beyond the arrogance and defensiveness you may feel, beyond all the self-protecting barriers of the ego, there awaits the discovery of your True Eternal Self. Begin by turning inward. Begin to increase your self-awareness.

Begin with this simple experiment:

On a day you choose, begin by looking at your reflection in a mirror. If this is not possible for some readers for any reason then use the creative power of your imagination. As you gaze on your physical image begin to notice all that is superficial. You will, no doubt, immediately judge what you see. Take the time and allow each judgment to be experienced. Some come quite quickly. Others will slowly be revealed.

Some judgments may be harsh: your nose is too big or too small, perhaps your eyes are slightly crossed or one ear is bigger than another. Your hair is turning gray or you think it should be a different color. Maybe you are balding. Notice all you see as an imperfection, all scars, all deformities.

Or perhaps you are pleased with what you see. You see such beauty. You take confidence in the allure of your physical body as you recall all those who desire to hold it. You judge what you see to be complete and perfect. You are satisfied by the physical image you see, pleased by its fleeting beauty. Whether you judge the body harshly or with great favor, it is still a judgment. Take the time to experience the thoughts you have of yourself. When you have grown tired of looking at the surface, at this image you present to the world, take a moment and say to yourself, "There is more to me than what I can see."

On the second day of this exercise, look again into the mirror, but this time resist any judgments. Look past the judgments made on how your body is formed. Realize only that you have eyes to see and a nose to smell, and a mouth so you can eat and speak, and ears so you may hear. Realize their function. Realize they have a practical use in the physical world.

Even if one or more of your physical senses should not be working, realize that even without them you continue to exist. You are still alive because you are more than a body. There is within you a life unending, a beautiful expression of God which has given the body its form and movement. Consider this flame of light, this eternal force dwelling within.

On the third day return to the mirror, again without any judgments. Look at your reflection and ask yourself, "Who am I really?"

Begin to consider how much you have tried to live up to other people's expectations. Begin to realize how you have formed an identity outside of your *True Self*. Examine how much of your self-image is determined by what you do for a living. See how you redefine yourself according to the demands of a career. Contemplate how much of your identity is created by what social groups you belong to, what segment of society you have found yourself a part of, whether it is of an economic, cultural, or racial interpretation.

Consider those limitations and realize you are more than a particular race, more than a member of a particular religious organization, more than the culture and society in which you were born. There is more. There is more for you to see.

On the fourth day of this experiment as you again look in the mirror, take notice of your face and body. Look without judgment. See yourself standing there alone, independent of the clothing and uniforms you've adopted. See yourself totally alone, removed from what people think of you, even separate from your own opinions about yourself. See yourself separate from your surroundings, no longer a creature of the earth.

Feel within yourself an emptiness. Do not be frightened by this empty feeling. You will experience it many times as old judgments are washed away by new understandings. Do not let the ego get confused. The emptiness you may feel is but a new beginning, a relinquishing of the old way so that a rebirth can occur. Continue to empty yourself of all self—imposed judgments. Be willing to sacrifice those judgments, good or bad. When you feel yourself casting off the beliefs of the ego, you will soon discover there is more to you than you have realized. There is so much more. There is an eternal part of your being, pure, wise, and strong. It dwells beneath the surface of your consciousness, rich in abilities, loving and patient.

On the fifth day you will need to be patient. Take the time, however long, to look upon yourself with a sense of curiosity, a sense of wonderment, as you gaze beyond your image in the mirror. Be aware of any feeling that may arise. Following emptiness, often there is sadness. This sinking feeling of depression is a period of mourning as you begin to sacrifice what you held to be so important for such a long time. Depression comes from a sense of loss.

For some people it can be quite severe. It may feel as if you were dying. In a way you are dying. You are experiencing a form of death. You feel the death of your former self. You feel the death of the ego. This is necessary because you are growing too big, too expansive, to be kept within the confines of such a small image you've had of yourself. You are putting aside the things of childhood to face a new maturity.

If you feel like crying, if you feel the death of your old self, go right ahead. Allow the tears to come, but do not try to resurrect the old self. Do not reach out to the past to recapture what used to be. Look forward.

Let the sadness be experienced, but remind yourself you are only removing an old piece of clothing that has become too tattered, too worn and torn to be of any further use. And in the sadness, as the tears flow, you must remind yourself that there is more to you. There is a great deal more for you to see. Let this thought of a new image and new understandings of yourself give hope. In this mourning period you say goodbye to the old identity, resisting any temptation to keep it alive by realizing it is no longer necessary for your survival.

On the sixth day stand before the mirror and see yourself clean and pure. See yourself purged of all that was old and useless. Yes, some of the old remains, but are slowly fading. A change of identity comes slowly. Self-realization is an on going process. It cannot be rushed.

But on this day you stand like a child naked to the world. Naked to yourself. There is a sense of being born again. You will discover new eyes to see, new ears to hear, new words whispering from your mouth. Sweet perfumes from beautiful flowers come to you. Holiness surrounds you.

This stage we call "born again," because all that was old and useless is dying off and you are willing to be born again with a new spirit, a new understanding of yourself and of life. As the limitations of the ego are relinquished you can begin to express your *True Personality*. You will recognize yourself as a part of God, and God as a part of you. As well, you will come to know spirituality as a real force in your life. Let this divine force cleanse you. Let it warm and protect you. Let it surround you because you have become as a little baby, one that is growing rapidly, but still needs the comfort and protection of something greater. You may feel vulnerable, as defenseless as a newborn, but know you are protected. Take comfort that you are not alone and there are spiritual forces gathering to support and encourage you.

As a newborn, you can look forward to what lies ahead. There is so much more to be seen, but it must be seen with new eyes. There is more to be heard, but with new ears. There is more for you to experience because you will have a new heart, a heart filled with love, with hope and with an enthusiasm for the new world that awaits you.

On the seventh day of this experiment you will be away from your image in the mirror. Instead, sit quietly in a comfortable room. This is a time of repose, a time to receive as you allow the realizations of the past six days to settle within your consciousness.

Sit in silence and be open to whatever may come to you. You may hear music though there is no radio playing. You may detect the scent of flowers though there are no flowers in the room. Relax and be open to receive.

Forces gather close to you imparting their gifts. Listen for their voices. Feel their embrace of peace. Accept their gift of love. Relax and feel the lightness of being which comes when freed from the chains of limitation. Put aside all cares and worries of the world and relax.

Take joy in the new body at rest. Appreciate your physical body for what it is. Know that it is just a vehicle for your *True Personality* to express itself in the world. Begin to realize that you have taken this form for a particular reason and it is a good reason even if you don't understand why. This human form you have taken for awhile is to assist you. It is not a hindrance. The physical body you've adopted is neither the gateway nor the obstacle to your happiness. Appreciate the body but do not make it important. Do not identify with it. On this seventh day put it aside and keep your attention on that which is real, that which is eternal and powerful.

Feel the spirit within you. Feel the force of God flowing in your life. Surrounded by this force you will walk lightly in this world. Know you are just passing by and beyond this world there is more, much more. Begin to look for the truth beyond physical form. Seek with enthusiasm, curiosity and expectation and you will find there is more to life than you imagined.

Beyond the ego consciousness and its struggles with the world there awaits the gifts of God. They are there for you to accept when you are ready. Accept these gifts and you will see yourself as a beautiful expression of God. You will discover you are complete and whole, perfect in love and joy.

Consider no longer looking outside yourself in search of what the ego thinks is missing. What has been missing all along was the freedom to allow your *True Personality* to come forth and greet the world. When it begins to do so you will find you lack nothing as the whole universe rushes in to support you.

Return to paradise. Return to the realm of spirit and know all has been given for your personal growth and understanding. Let the forces of God become a part of your life and bring you a joy and love not found in the world.

As you continue with this book, as new discoveries are made and joy enters you heart, know there is more. There is more for you to feel and experience. Life does not stop. Creation has no end. You will continue to grow into a new awareness that leads to new understanding that leads to an even greater awareness. There is always something waiting to be discovered, always something to enhance who you are and enrich your experiences on earth. Why else would you linger in the world unless there was more to learn?

Take this experiment we have given you and use it, as you will. A single day can take weeks, months or longer. Each day is a step towards understanding. What you feel will be felt many times as you approach a new direction in life and enter into the transition of emptiness, then emerge with a greater understanding. Take your time, as much as you need. Maybe for some people it will be a few minutes. For others it may take many hours or days or years. In this there is no judgment. It is how individuals differ in the world. However long it takes keep searching for that spark of realization that there is more to you than what the world will have you believe. Search for the light of your *True Personality*. You will know it when you find it.

# Chapter 6

## Conflict

There comes a stage in spiritual development when you will experience the conflict between the fears of the ego and the power of spirit. During this stage of conflict you will feel as if you are teeter—tottering between the two. One moment spirituality is in the forefront. The next moment it is the ego dominating your thoughts and actions. Your *True Personality* is coming forth into your consciousness and is a more powerful vibration than the ego. As your *True Self* emerges it will challenge how you think, how you see the world and how you live your life. As spiritual awareness begins to grow stronger the ego will begin to diminish. The ego has no power against the higher vibrations of your *True Self*, but it will resist. This time of conflict will be a time of fear and confusion as the ego struggles to survive.

An ego-based identity seeks only that which strengthens it. All else is seen as a threat. Therefore, in the beginning, as you take the next step in evolution, you will feel a conflict, a division within yourself as a new way of being struggles to emerge. This is an important and beneficial awakening. Be patient, but also be strong.

It will be a great temptation to go back to what is familiar. The ego will seek that which is known, that which it sees as safe. Even a painful life is preferable to the ego than having to face the unknown. During times of conflict the ego retreats into the familiarity of old beliefs and routine actions, while the *True Self* instinctually moves forward towards new experiences, new understandings, and a new way of being in the world. Conflict arises during these periods of transition as you move from the past into the future, uncertain of the next step.

Realize it is the ego causing the uncertainty, the confusion and conflict. It struggles against that which it cannot control. This period of conflict will last only as long as you cling to the old way of being. It is a battle, to be sure, but the inner struggle is but a birth into a new awareness. You will face this struggle many times as you reach new levels of awareness and your *True Self* radiates its power. There will be conflict each time another old belief cherished by the ego is to be sacrificed. Do not fear these conflicts. They are the birth pains of self-transformation.

The trials of conflict will come in stages, as much as you can handle at a time. It cannot be rushed. Take small steps in the beginning. Be kind to yourself during these times of emotional turmoil. Take time to rest and take the time to sit quietly. Take time to call on those spiritual forces that aid you in this struggle. You do not go through this alone.

Peace will come to you again, but the lesson is not over. Once the initial distress of conflict subsides there is an attempt to compromise. This is a time when the ego will try to take what spiritual knowledge you have gained and make it its own. It will take the new knowledge and apply it to the old way of being. To illustrate: rather than exchanging an old shirt for a new one, the ego will take the sparkling clean shirt and place it over the old tattered one. You cannot take the knowledge you are gaining, the new insights and the joy you are feeling and layer it over the ego. It will only be an illusion.

Outside the appearance is spiritual, the words spoken sound spiritual, even the show of psychic ability seems evidence of having become a spiritual being. Beneath the surface, however, the ambitions, the fears, the quest for personal power still remain. The ego maintains control. Be aware of this within yourself. Be aware of such compromises in others; those who seek to appear special in the world, those who use their spiritual knowledge to gain personal power, to accumulate material wealth, to attract attention and adulation, those who see all "rewards" as proof of divine favor. Such individuals often form the more dogmatic, exclusive forms of organized religion where "they teach as doctrine the precepts of men."

This is not to be judged, but seen as an essential step in evolution. It is a valuable experience. Since the vibrations of spiritual consciousness and egotistical thought patterns are different and incompatible, inevitably an even greater conflict results and the individual will be forced to choose a new direction. Conflict has its value.

It is during the mental confusion and emotional turmoil that the differences between the *True Personality* and the ego become obvious. Become aware of the conflict. Understand the dynamics of personal growth. Know that as the ego begins to weaken it will struggle to gain prominence. Anger and fear and depression may increase. Confusion results because the ego cannot understand what is happening. It is too limited.

As the ego fights to regain its position you will find yourself thinking only of yourself, attempting to glorify your achievements of newfound knowledge that you are only beginning to glimpse. This is a trick of the ego. This is an attempt by the ego to take what is universal and make it personal. During this time you must be your most disciplined and ever vigilant.

Do not judge yourself, but simply be aware and learn. Take time to question the ego's influence on your spiritual life. Some thoughts may be quite subtle, convincing you that what you want is of a spiritual nature, whereas, it appeals more to the ego than to the heart. Simply remember the criteria of the ego. Remember its need for self-preservation, its concerns with physical well-being, and its hunger for personal power. If your thoughts are centered on fear and worry and self-defense, know it is of the ego. If you wish to glorify yourself to the world, it is of the ego.

Because you are still a child you may not recognize the ego at work. Therefore, carefully take small steps. The beginning of spiritual awareness may seem wobbly. You may be unsure which foot to put forward. You may easily fall. But if you are sincere in your desire for spiritual growth there will be someone to catch you. You will again have the opportunity to stand and walk.

Allow yourself times of conflict. They are growing pains. Allow yourself to fail at times. You will learn from the experience. On this path of evolution be willing to stumble and fall. Be willing to again stand up and walk. A child is willing to crawl before learning to walk. A child does not give up should he or she fall. The child continues to learn as helping hands support the attempt. Soon the child learns to run. So it is with spiritual evolution.

And, as you stand and take the next step forward, be aware of outside distractions. Old situations, old attitudes and even old friends will rise up to lead you astray. You are taking a new path, but the old way is still visible, still strong and demanding. Do not judge it. Instead, understand it for what it is, nothing more than the past pulling at you. Find the strength to walk in a new direction. Be willing to stand-alone for a moment, and then ask the forces of God to help you take the next step.

Periods of conflict do not last long, but they are a crucial time in your development. If you seek to avoid conflict by being lazy, if you are satisfied with your present self, if you think there is nothing left to learn, then you are a child content to crawl, never knowing the joy of running.

Dear child, keep in mind this is only the beginning. Be mindful that there is much more to life and do not settle for less. A great deal awaits you but first this bridge of conflict must be crossed. Ignore the raging waters beneath it. Become deaf to the voices calling behind you, calling you to return.

Dear child of great strength, do not allow your legs to collapse beneath you, but continue to cross the bridge of conflict regardless of the difficulties. Continue to keep your mind and vision on the other side awaiting you. This will help. This will offer encouragement.

As you cross the bridge you will see and feel your spiritual power. This will encourage you to face the conflict and endure the turmoil. Tell yourself at this time you will not turn back. Tell yourself that you will not leave the road because something glitters off to the side. It is only a distraction appealing to the ego. Tell yourself that as you move into a new consciousness, as you move into a new way of being, God is with you. You are not alone. You have never been alone.

What you seek is far greater than anything you have ever known. There is nothing in the past that can possibly describe where you are going. No past experience will explain the new person you will soon discover within yourself.

You are learning. Keep that in mind as you stumble and fall; you are learning. Keep in mind when you are tempted and become distracted that you are learning. Give yourself the gift of compassion. Give yourself a sense of grace. Remind yourself you have chosen this way and you have the power to accomplish it. During times of conflict and confusion you will find a strength you did not know you had; strength you kept hidden, strength unknown by the world around you. Ask for this strength and it will rise up within you.

## Chapter 7

# Serving Two Masters

As your spiritual awareness begins to grow realize there is so much more to learn. Do not pat yourself on the back for every small achievement. As we have stated, there is so much more for you to do, so much more for you to discover. You get a tiny peek at spiritual reality and you think it is a great big picture. You will be discovering more. You will come to greater understandings quicker than ever before. Remember all we have told you so far is real. We have not come to confuse you. You confuse yourself enough without our help.

At this time you are still taking small steps towards realizing a greater sense of self. The ego, however, is still a powerful influence and sees these small steps as its own achievement. When this occurs it is the individual's attempt to serve two masters. As Jesus taught, it is impossible to serve two masters, as you will come to love one and hate the other.

You cannot be pulled apart. You cannot be divided. Serving the ego is to serve one master. To serve your *True Self* is to serve another master. Ego and the *True Self* are two different masters, two different ways of being.

You must begin to acknowledge the distinction between the two in your life. You must also understand that during this period of time, as you begin the first steps along the spiritual path, the ego will insist that it alone is the only master. It will try to tell you what you should do, what you should think and how you should act in accordance with how things have been done in the past.

In its attempt to remain dominant, the ego will either deny the message of this book, or, as with some individuals, the ego will try to pretend that spirituality is a desire of the ego. An individual will convince himself or herself that the ego can be used to achieve spiritual enlightenment. This is not so.

We remind you that the ego is concerned only with physical survival and cannot fully comprehend the majesty and beauty of spiritual reality. Do not be alarmed by this, but take time to reflect, time to look inward. The ego's way to harness spirituality is by making it a project; a goal to achieve, which can then be organized and converted into a system of dogmatic beliefs. The ego will intellectualize spirituality and in doing so will limit its greatness.

Deeper within your being, however, is the desire of your heart to seek light where once there was only darkness, to bring love into the world, to transform yourself into a spiritual force in the universe, not for your own glory, but for the sake of your soul and the souls of others. Spirituality is who you are not what you can do.

Already you may have begun to experience an awakening of your spiritual power, especially if you have taken the time to do the simple exercises, especially if you have made the effort to look within and examine your life. Even if the awakening is only a spark of excitement about the possibilities that await you, it is enough.

As well, you may begin to experience an increase in awareness and intuition. Such abilities are but tools used to manifest your spiritual *True Self*. Even within the egotistical way of being you can have what are known as "psychic episodes," but what is psychic and what is spiritual is not necessarily the same. Each person has the ability within his or her consciousness to see beyond the three dimensions of this world. Every person has intuitive abilities that can be used to various degrees. Such abilities are not to be confused with the true nature of spirituality.

The ego will tell you quite adamantly that it is the same. The ego will tell you that because you can see this and you can perceive that, then you are being spiritual. This is not true. You can stay on that level, if you wish. You can think you have achieved something great because you are intuitive, because people say you are psychic, but that will limit your development. You will never come to greater understandings if you are willing to settle for such a small glimpse of reality.

If you want more in life then keep walking. Keep crossing the bridge of conflict as you leave the past behind and step towards the still-to-be-discovered realm of spirituality. Should this be confusing to you, should you feel overwhelmed by the battle between the ego and the spiritual, simply put your hand on the center of your chest, and take a deep breath. Quiet your mind of all thoughts going in and out of your head. In that quiet moment you may achieve a degree of confidence to help you take the next step. In the quiet of your heart you will discover the strength needed to switch your allegiance to another master.

During this early development, as you try to move away from the ego, as you try to find something more meaningful in your life, there is often the temptation to take one step forward, then stand perfectly still and enjoy the victory of that one step. Realize that after taking one step there is another step to take and after that still another. It is much too slow to take a single step then come to a standstill. It is the fears of the ego that have you cautiously making your way forward.

Should this be the case, should you be satisfied to stand still in wonder and awe at the baby steps you've taken, something will come along to push you forward, some event will nudge you to continue along the path. There is nothing in the universe that stands still. You are no exception. The ego seeks security of settling in one place, adopting a stance, and protecting that position. Life means growth and change. Life means you keep walking.

This is when discipline comes in. This is where the strength you already have within you must come forward for it is at this time when people who experience a little bit of spiritual reality are willing to be satisfied and not go any further. It is also at this point that people often reach for a spiritual experience in their life, then retreat into the old way of being because it is familiar, because it is the way they have always done things and because they still find value in the past. Such people are willing to settle for less.

It is so much like the time when you were a child just beginning to go to school. You went into the classroom with no idea of what you were going to be taught. No one expected you to know the lessons beforehand. Life is like a classroom. You must go in with an open mind, and an open heart, and be willing to learn. Be willing, therefore, to have experiences that will teach you and further your education, further the progress in your evolution. If you enter a classroom thinking you already have all the answers you might as well pack up and go home because the poor teacher will not be able to tell you a thing. So, don't be afraid to take the next step, admitting you do not know what lies ahead, but willing to find out.

You must go beyond the ego's fears of the unknown. As we have already stated, the ego is too limited in its perceptions to offer any real insight into what life is all about. The ego has always seen a distorted reflection of true reality. Even the image you have of yourself is not who you truly are. You are more than a body and a mind. Be willing to come into the classroom to learn, to discover, to grow into the person God created you to be: a child of light and love.

Listen to the new master within you. Listen for the spiritual forces surrounding you who have come to guide and encourage you along the path of awakening. You have entered a new classroom and there stands before you a new master. As in any classroom, with each new endeavor, you must be disciplined. In the beginning you must work very hard. You must be willing to sacrifice the time spent in the idle pursuits of the ego so that you can learn.

If you do not want this then you should close the book. If you are not willing to heed the voice of a new master then put this book away. It will not do you any good. The information given so far can help, but the person reading this must take responsibility for his or her own life. You must take the information and integrate it and become one with each and every word on this page.

This may frighten some people. They will think they are being influenced. They are afraid to give up their identity because a new master comes forward asking them to trust. Yet they are willing to heed the voice of the old master, the ego that fears losing control. If you are one of these people then put the book down. You will learn some other way. This message cannot help you. It can help only as much as you will allow. A teacher can give information, but if you are not listening, if you do not want to do your homework, if you do not want to take responsibility, what more can the poor teacher do? Do not waste your time.

However, if in this time of conflict, if during the times of confusion when the ego is getting very weak, but still trying to lead you off the path, if you are tempted to return to the old and useless but can still feel the desire to change your life then continue. If you desire to learn more about yourself, if you seek to discover the true purpose of life, if you yearn to share in the eternal mysteries, then keep reading, keep walking. Be a good student and work hard.

Now is the time to gather your strength. Now is the time you must make the decision as to which master you are going to serve. You must sacrifice the old master. **You must sacrifice the power of the ego.** It has served you for a limited time and now let it go. Push it gently aside, or with great force if need be. A new voice calls to you. It calls you to a new life.

The master Jesus has taught that you cannot put new wine into an old bottle. This teaching has confused many people; those who did not want to hear what he truly meant. In order to become "born again" in the true sense, in order to discover your true spiritual self, in order to leave behind the sorrow and struggle of your world, you must be willing to change. Do not, therefore, take this new information given to you and put it into an old bottle or this new information, like wine, will sour. Allow yourself to be a sparkling clean, a new and strong bottle so these words like sweet wine can be poured into you and fill you up. Now is the time to begin. Now is the time to sacrifice.

So has the Buddha taught; you must sacrifice the desires of this world to realize Nirvana. This has also been misunderstood. Nirvana is a state of being and that state of being is the spiritual awakening of an individual who has sacrificed the fears of the ego and the limitations of a self-centered identity. Nirvana is being your *True Self.* You are Nirvana. You become Nirvana when you walk away from the old desires, those ambitions and fears never satisfied because they are of the ego, because they are the limited goals of the world.

Ask yourself what causes so much conflict and pain in your life? Ask yourself, why are you so willing to hold on to those things? Ask yourself, what sacrifices are you to make?

All we are asking is for you to remove the burden of fear. We ask you to sacrifice the heaviness of pain, the suffocation of selfish ambition, the chains of anger towards yourself and others. We ask you to relinquish the limited concept you have of love in order to discover a true eternal love, in order to discover an inner joy, in order to discover a true relationship of sharing between yourself and others.

Such a small sacrifice to make. Yet, you don't want to discard the old master because you think the ego is who you are. This is not true. You are more than that. Keep walking. Do not stand still. There is still a long way to go, but you have reached the most difficult part. At this point along the path there are stumbling blocks that threaten to trip you. At this stage there are obstacles to be conquered. During this time of conflict as you turn from one master to heed another voice, there are barricades to your development that must be faced and surmounted. The ego will see such challenges as overwhelming and even impossible. Your *True Personality* guided by a new master will find the power to prevail.

So, dear child, as you take your first steps be vigilant. Be aware of what is in front of you. It is difficult to walk forward if you are looking behind at what use to be. The first steps can be troublesome, but you can cross this bridge. It can be done. If in your heart you feel the enthusiasm and the excitement in discovering the light that dwells within, then you will make it.

The new master calls to you. Heed the voice and step boldly forward.

# Chapter 8

## The Power of Decision

During times of conflict, during times of emotional upheaval, what is important to realize is those events which bring such distress are asking you to make a decision. During times of conflict you stand at a crossroads in life. One road continues on as if nothing has happened. It is the safe and familiar road. The other road leads in a new direction. It is a narrow road and may be difficult to see at first. Old beliefs may blind you to the road's existence. The ego will deny it. Nevertheless, events have altered the course of your life and a new path opens before you. A decision must be made.

Sometimes the decision to be made is obvious. Often times you must first clear away the emotional turmoil before the choice becomes apparent. It may be a confusing time. It may be painful. But you have the strength within you to overcome the conflict. The strength comes from making a decision as to how you want to live in the world.

What causes the confusion is the ego's inability to cope with certain situations. Feelings of helplessness and fear and anger arise, as the ego's survival mechanism proves useless. It is fear which clouds judgment. It is anger that restricts perception. It is loss of control that induces feelings of weakness and helplessness.

What needs to be understood is that each conflict is a stepping-stone in your evolution. Each conflict forces you to reconsider your definition of yourself and reality. The emotional disturbance necessitates a change of direction. With each episode of strife and dissension, with each emotional and mental struggle, there is a decision to be made. Often it is a difficult decision that awaits. Often it is a decision that will change your life.

It is through your decisions that you will discover your power and creative force. It is a small way to realize you are the determining force in your life. But first you must realize there are no right and no wrong decisions. Whatever you decide will lead you along a particular course that will teach you. It is only the ego, out of fear, that presents the dilemma of right or wrong. The ego fears failure. Failure to the ego means death of the self. This causes unnecessary confusion and only postpones making a decision.

Because of this fear of failure, some individuals settle for indecision by not choosing anything at all. Instead, they are willing to surrender their power by having another make decisions for them. Some individuals unable to cope with crises, unable to take any personal responsibility, will prefer to simply leave it "in God's hands." We must point out that even indecision is a calculated decision. You have decided upon a course of action called indecision. You have chosen to be in limbo.

The unfortunate result of choosing to be indecisive is you will continue to lose power while hiding in the grayness of irresponsibility. Nothing in creation can stand still; events will force you into taking a different course of action. Events will force you to realize that indecision is an attempt at avoidance. You can then begin again to take responsibility for yourself.

When you accept the power of your decisions you begin to acknowledge and accept responsibility for whatever consequences may follow. Whether the consequences of a decision is seen as good, bad or indifferent, it must be accepted as a result of your own decision. If you feel a course of action is perhaps hindering your highest good, simply acknowledge you have made that decision, take responsibility for the consequences of that decision, then choose another course of action.

Realize that life is just not thrust upon you. The events in your life do not occur out of a void. Everything that happens to you has a meaning, has a lesson that brings further wisdom. By coming into an earthly existence you willingly decided to participate in all that may occur during a particular lifetime. You chose to learn the lessons of those specific experiences. Therefore, do not allow the events of the past when your ego felt overwhelmed and helpless keep you powerless. You always have the power to make a decision. Be willing to make the necessary decisions. Be willing to take responsibility for your actions. Be willing to change the direction of your life through the decisions you make.

Should you choose to develop your spiritual self, should you seek to discover your *True Personality*, strength will be needed. What occurs every time you make a decision to move in a new direction is similar to separating two magnets. You are one of those magnets. When you decide to move away from the limitations of the ego, you pull away from a magnetic field. If you have ever pulled one magnet away from another you know the greatest strength is needed for the initial separation.

It is not until you reach a certain distance that you will no longer feel the magnetic pull of the past. Therefore, when making the decision to leave one way of being, that is, the magnetic field of past decisions, and attempt to enter another way of being, a great deal of strength, determination, and discipline is required.

Try the experiment of our illustration by placing two magnets together so their energy currents are in alignment and they are joined as one. This represents the decisions you have made which attracted those experiences harmonizing with your thoughts, feelings, and actions determined by the ego. As you pull them apart feel the force needed to draw the magnets away from each other. This represents your decision to seek a new way of being in the world, a new way free from the past, free from the limitations of the ego.

At this stage in your evolution you are also pulling away from the force of a magnetic field and experiencing the pull it has upon you. It is no coincidence that the magnetic field of the ego is exerting an enormous force upon you just as you begin to take the next step. The events that occur at this time, the people in your life, the attractions of the world, will pull even harder at you. The ego realm will seem so much stronger than ever before. However, with increased awareness, the pull of the ego will be obvious.

The blatant attempt to hold you back should serve as an aid, rather than a hindrance in helping you make a decision. Observe how yearnings for past pleasures grow stronger; the need for a certain food, a new article of clothing, and in some cases the physical urges for drugs or alcohol will seem more insistent than ever before. Unless you are aware that the ego is attempting to assert itself you may be discouraged. If you cannot conquer these urges it is best to give in, but not give up. Stumble and fall, but rise again. Each time you will gain strength and awareness.

Be patient with yourself, but be strong. Be patient with others. Now is not the time to concern yourself with other egos for it is important you concentrate on your own evolution. Later in life you may be asked to help those struggling to learn and grow. Always have great compassion for those around you who are still within the magnetic field of ego even those who attempt to call you back into the past. Have compassion, but be strong. Be aware that all your experiences so far echo the past and the magnetic field of past decisions will keep pulling at you. Be aware and be strong.

There is strength in the power of decision. By reading the words of this book, by your own searching for meaning in your life, by considering the possibility of a new way of being, you have already made the mental decision to take the next step. Now, at this very moment, is when the emotions must follow. The emotional stage of making a decision is the one aspect of decision-making often forgotten. Most people make the mental decision, and then attempt to put it into immediate action. Few take the time to consider their emotional commitment to a decision.

Every decision, even those that may be small and appear insignificant, alters the course of your life. The ego fears that a wrong decision will bring failure and failure is a threat to survival. The ego will instead channel the power of decision towards concerns that are safe and inconsequential; what to wear, what to eat, what is entertaining, what employment seems the most secure and financially rewarding. In this the ego directs the power of decision towards externals. Even in these things the ego will agonize about possible failure.

Fears of failure, fear of losing power, fear of being seen as foolish, have determined the ego's decisions. These emotional conflicts have influenced many an individual's course in life. Therefore, in making the decision to take the next step in your evolution, you may still feel the fear, but don't trust it. Beyond the emotional turmoil there is wisdom. Such wisdom is within you. It comes from a calm and balanced place within your consciousness. When the emotional turmoil has passed, when you are at peace and can see a situation clearly, then you can bring the three aspects of making a decision into accord.

Remember that the ego will only make decisions that will protect it regardless of the consequences to others. The ego's decisions are always based on changing what it fears, changing what is outside itself. No matter how often external circumstances may change, the basic fears of the ego remain. Understand that what is being asked of you is an emotional commitment to seek greater understandings, to bring your mind, your heart and your actions into accord with the decision you must make to transcend limitations.

The true power of decision brings about personal transformation. When the three elements of making a decision are in accord, when the mind, the heart, and the willingness to put the decision into action are in agreement, the power of decision proves itself to be an enormous creative force changing whom you are and your perceptions of reality. The power of your decision will effect a change to the extent where your magnetic vibration evolves to a higher frequency. When your mind is willing to turn towards a new direction, when you are emotionally at peace with that decision and begin to put it into action then the power within you will change your experience of life. Without the emotional commitment to your decision all actions will be crippled.

If hesitation, doubt, and fear are allowed to remain, then it will weaken the decision. When this happens, when the emotions are at odds with the mental decision, the power of your decision is diminished. If you attempt to separate one magnet from another, but are afraid to do so, your actions will be tentative at a time when all your strength is needed. Those who have allowed fear and hesitation to influence their search for spiritual reality are quickly pulled back into the magnetic field of the ego and have dismissed spirituality as a failure. Some individuals think spirituality should be revealed in spite of their doubts. But, it is fear that has made them blind. It is their own fear that has limited their experience. The magnetic pull of the ego proved stronger than their desire to learn.

As you pull away from the magnetic field of the ego realize you can not allow it to make all your decisions, even if some decisions made in the past had at one time brought you pleasure. The attraction of past experiences must be sacrificed. Only then can the emotions be brought into agreement with your decision to move forward and evolve. It is the emotions and their attachment to memories of the past that hold you back.

Because you have decided that certain experiences of the past have been pleasurable or that a certain way of being in the world has helped you to survive, you continue to cling to the past. This limits your growth. If only you would realize that what happened yesterday, what happened last year, what happened when you were a baby, is now gone and cannot be recaptured. Just try to think logically for a moment and realize the past no longer exists except in your memory.

Even though you constantly try to recreate those moments of happiness in your life, it could never quite be the same. This will only lead to frustration, and a growing sense of emptiness. When the pain of frustration and emptiness is felt keenly within you then a new decision must be made. Sometimes, especially in the beginning, depression must first be experienced as an individual faces the emotional limitations of the ego.

Depression is often the initial stage of separation within the self. Sadness and confusion of thought results when the mind is determined to go one way, but your emotions have remained trapped in the past. In this you are trying to serve two masters, as stated in the previous chapter.

Simply be aware and acknowledge the inner conflict between the mind and the emotions. Have those experiences of depression, frustration and emptiness, if you must, but also consider how you have gone through life repeating past patterns, clinging to old routines and cherishing old beliefs. Observe the frustration of repeating a certain course of action simply because it worked at one time in the past and you expect it to work again. Many individuals who have tried with great determination to stay in the past, to keep the past alive and drag it into the future will often become quite bitter and disappointed in the latter part of their lives.

Others have become lost in what used to be. The power of their memories has become so strong that the present and future no longer exist. Life comes to a standstill. Activity becomes repetitious. Growth becomes severely limited. Death is the eventual release from such a prison. Then do they come to the realization that what they once had no longer exists. It is gone.

In your own life there have been experiences that you have tried to turn into a lifestyle. You had experiences that you use to judge all other experiences because in that one past moment you felt happy and satisfied. In that one brief moment your ego was pleased. You have also had events in your life that have caused pain and sorrow; those you carry as a burden. You still allow those past experiences to affect the way you walk in the world.

Realize how short-lived each event was; all things pass. Your existence on earth is temporary. The moments in your life are brief. You cannot change and you cannot recreate the past. True satisfaction is not found in a single moment. It is eternal and with you always. If you felt true love just once in your life you would not have to go searching for it again. It would remain with you always. The ego, limited by time and space, focused on externals and by constantly looking outside itself seeks situations similar to those past moments when it was satisfied, when it felt happiness, when it had a glimpse of love, or a sense of being powerful. By seeking these feelings through outside influences you will be searching again and again. That which is outside yourself will change; brief moments that come and go. The pleasures of the ego will always be short— lived.

The demands of the ego for satisfaction is unending as it continues to search for those experiences which give it pleasure. The frustration you feel from time to time comes from having the demands of the ego denied for even a moment. Emptiness is felt when the repetition of your actions, unable to meet the high standards of the past, become dull and meaningless. Depression rises when your ego reveals its powerlessness, when all it has held dear, all it cherished, all it counted on for survival is suddenly gone.

You have come to a crossroads in life. At that moment in time you must make a decision to move forward and face the unknown. Let the past remain in the past. Have faith that you are not leaving behind that which seems safe and secure, only to fall into darkness and danger. Much more awaits you. A stronger force calls out to you. That force is unlike the dictatorship of the ego. It whispers in a gentle voice trying to get your attention. But it is you who must decide. It is you who chooses to listen.

You are not being asked to leave behind the essential desires so intrinsic to the human existence. The need for happiness, the quest for satisfaction, the quest for a sense of self and the important desire to experience love will remain. It is how you choose to meet those desires that must be decided upon.

When the Buddha taught about removing all desires of this world, he revealed that the way to satisfy those needs is not through the ego, for such solutions are temporary, but to seek the way of the spirit. Once those desires are satisfied through the efforts of your *True Personality* and your spiritual connection to God, they will no longer be desires. They will be reality. You can only desire what you do not have; once you possess true joy and true love they are yours forever.

This is what the next step promises you. You may think this is impossible. It is because of past experiences you have never known true satisfaction. You may think the promise of a true, eternal love unbelievable because you have yet to feel it. However, if you will just continue to move towards God, towards true spirituality, towards a new way of being in the world, then you can discover the true meaning of satisfaction.

Up until now you could not understand. It has not been a part of your experience, so far. You can begin to understand now. Realize there is a way of being still unknown to you. It can be a part of your existence. It will be revealed if you decide it is something you want.

You have spent many years in ego. To pull away takes discipline. Decide to take responsibility for your life and you will find the strength to move beyond the past. Be willing to sacrifice. Be willing to let go of all that which no longer serves you. Be willing to remove the blindfold so you can see a new way of being. Faith will overcome fear. Strength will overcome weakness. Decide to take the next step. Decide now and you will begin to see a greater reality.

# Chapter 9

▼

# Strength

Through your decisions you will find your strength. By making decisions you acknowledge the creative power in your life. Know you can decide the course of your life and you begin to discover within you the awakening of spiritual strength. This strength is an inner power that can never be lost. It is with you at all times. It is persuasive and persevering when needed, and it can be quite forceful should the necessity arise.

The strength we speak of is so unlike the world's definition of strength. The world would have you think strength is based upon the ability of the physical body to survive, to assert itself and to protect itself against threats real or imagined. Fear of loss, fear of being weak, fear of destruction underlies the ego's quest for strength. The seemingly endless struggle for personal power and strength between individuals, between races and religions, and between nations, is still the ego's primitive fight for survival.

Even against its own creation, this place beneath your feet called earth, humanity attempts to conquer the forces of nature, asserting the ego's will against a force that will always prove greater. The earth is older than mankind. It existed before humanity took its present form. Nature will always be stronger because it is wiser. The earth will prove its wisdom as landmasses shift, weather patterns alter, and winds and water overcome all obstacles. It is a matter of time. The history of your planet has shown this.

On a personal level, an individual seeks strength through physical prowess, through wealth, by enhancing sexual appeal, by creating competitiveness, and by seeking personal benefits regardless of the pain and suffering inflicted on others. This has become so much a part of your world that it is accepted as a natural expression of human endeavor. All these aspects of personal power, however, are distortions created by a limited awareness. Again, we say, the sole purpose of the ego is self-protection. The ego's attempts at strength is to maintain separation through physical force by driving away anything it cannot control, anything which threatens it's security, anything which challenges of dominance in human awareness. In its struggle to survive, the ego holds within the human consciousness all its fears, all its pains and sufferings. The ego's quest for personal power is born out of the inner turmoil its insecurity.

Like a house built on sand, the ego's concept of strength is unreliable. It is always insecure. There will always be another individual who proves to be more powerful. There will always be a nation better equipped for war. New technologies become more deadly. Governments change, empires collapse, economics are in constant fluctuation; you do not have to look far into the past to see this is so. The universe is constantly in transformation.

The ego fears such changes, feels powerless against them. Your *True Self*, however, has the wisdom that accepts change as an impetus of growth. Within your own life you have experienced the strength needed to accept change. After all, your own body went through various changes in order to grow. There would be little value in remaining an infant. You cannot stand still. Change is inevitable. You have the strength within you to face the changes that will bring about your own evolution.

Once you have decided to move along the path away from the ego to a more spiritual way of life, great strength will be needed. The ego will offer stubbornness against change when it is actually perseverance to move forward that needs to be called upon. The ego will offer anger to assert itself, when it is actually a calm, steady frame of mind that will suffice. And the ego will offer up all its fears and insecurities that endanger the physical body, when in truth, the forcefulness of your inner strength will protect you.

Become aware of these differences, become aware that you must begin to make even more decisions about which strength you will seek. Know at this time that the old concepts of strength will not serve you. They will actually hinder your evolution. The ego's concept of strength comes from feeling insecure, whereas, true strength comes from feeling confident. This confidence is truly knowing who you are and trusting the power of God in your life.

You can now call into your life a new assistance, a new vibration known as inner strength. This is not a strength you must prove to others. You must prove it only to yourself. Those who have found this kind of strength keep it to themselves. They do not have to flaunt it. They do not have to test it. They are confident at all times that this strength is within them and it is there for their own use. It exists for them to help with all aspects of physical existence as well as to cultivate their spiritual abilities.

Those who have obtained spiritual strength regard each situation they face with a greater awareness. With a heightened intuitive ability they can decide accurately the wiser course of action and can move forward without hesitation. That is the purpose of inner strength. Such an ability does not have to be developed, does not have to be exercised and you do not have to test it. For now, all you have to do is acknowledge that it exists within you. Feel it within you. Learn to seek that inner strength, rather than be tempted into using the old way.

During this initial stage in your journey you may feel vulnerable. As you pull away from the ego it's likely you will feel threatened and find yourself being defensive even about trivial matters. In the old way of doing things you would have called upon the ego to protect you. In truth, you need no protection. The truth is, inner strength must rise up and guide you through these troubled times.

The ego cannot understand this. The ego would never rely upon something so invisible as inner strength. Instead, it relies upon armor to protect itself. It trusts in anger to get its point across. It seeks weapons to fight off any threats. It learns to hide. It does these things to protect the physical body, but this is not strength. The ego disregards the spiritual forces that are also available. It denies the power of the soul working in the material world.

The *True Self* finds its strength by trusting the force of God, trusting that force as an active power throughout the universe. It trusts true awareness and its intuitive capabilities to properly evaluate any given situation in life. Once you know the truth, what is there to fear? Nothing can destroy you. Life is eternal. Once you can see beyond the limitations of the ego, once you hear the voices of the spiritual powers that surround you, once you speak with clarity and knowledge, inner strength is yours. What need is there for protection? The ego that sets up barriers, which encloses you in its shield of protection, also keeps you from experiencing this spiritual reality.

When old fears diminish, when old wounds are healed, when you begin to seek a greater understanding than what the ego can provide, then true knowledge will come. Inner strength increases with this knowledge. It is a gift from your *True Personality*. It will lead to a righteous way of being putting you in harmony with the multitude of spiritual forces that surround you.

We understand that the word "righteousness" has been misused. The ego has claimed it as its own. What the ego has done is taken stubbornness, given it a moral justification, and called it righteousness. This is misguided. Righteousness is merely acknowledging the power of light over the power of the shadows. True righteousness is acknowledging the force of God in your life, rather than the terrified squealing of the ego. Spiritual righteousness is born out of love, not judgment.

Righteousness comes from the desire of the soul for all separation to end. This righteousness, and the strength which comes from it, is not found by putting on blinders that further narrows your vision. Instead, it is the result of taking away those beliefs that blind you. Only when you go beyond limited thinking can you see true beauty, true compassion, and true wisdom. Righteousness comes when you are no longer willing to settle for anything less.

When you are able to see the beauty of creation and your heart fills with joy, at the same time you may be saddened that others cannot see such a wonder, cannot see the power of God's creativity working throughout the universe. You may feel the urge to criticize those who will not see, those who will not hear, those who will not try. You may be tempted to judge, to point an accusing finger and point out the error of their ways. Should this happen to you, and it often does happen to those who have first started upon the path of self discovery, then pray it passes quickly. Do not judge others. To do so will only blind you. It is the ego that judges. The *True Self* seeks only to understand. Be strong, but be compassionate. Be righteous, but do not judge. Through your own inner strength you will remember when there was a time you were blind, a time when you relied only upon the ego.

Your inner strength will help you see this and other things clearly. It will guide you along the path so your footing is sure and steady. Your own inner strength will keep you from wandering off, will keep you from being trapped at a dead end and it will keep you from falling off cliffs. By your own decision to seek greater awareness and the inner strength that comes from that decision, you will overcome any obstacles that are placed before you by the world.

Use your inner strength as a compass along this spiritual journey. It will help you walk in the right direction. You shall fear no evil once you have this strength. Shadows of past fears will no longer frighten you. The egos of those around you will have no effect. Ridicule from the world will not deter you. Insults from those who judge cannot slow your progress.

Yes, there may be times you feel as if you are standing all alone especially when searching deep within your own being. But you are never alone. All that is good, all that is righteous, all that is of God will stand by you. Find strength in that knowledge. Your own determination will also lead you into relationships with others in the world who will stand by your side, walk with you, encourage you and keep you from those who would pull you back into the past. Of course, you are there for them as well. As you evolve, as your personal vibration alters, you will attract those of a similar vibration; anger attracts anger, weakness attracts weakness, and spirit attracts spirit.

The powerful strength of your spirit is greater than you realize. You will only come to know and experience this strength once the influence of the ego is sacrificed. At this stage in your journey we will give to you three items, three gifts of the spirit, which will help you to realize true inner strength. Take these gifts as we describe them. Take them into your awareness and make them your own. In your hand we place a fan. In your other hand we place a staff. Around your waist we hang a sword. Take a moment to visualize each gift. They are symbols, but can be made real in your life.

First see and feel the fan held in your hand. This fan is called, "gentle strength." You can use it to calm yourself during times of stress. It can also be used as a soft tap on your shoulder when you attention begins to wander, when you thoughts center on people and events that are really not your concern. With a few waves of the fan you can brush aside petty distractions. With a bit more force it can be used to deflect the energy of small annoyances, such as the critical thoughts of others directed your way. A gentle strength can be quite effective when used properly.

In your other hand you hold a staff. Again, visualize and feel how solid it is in your hand. See and feel the tip of the staff touching the ground. This staff is the strength of perseverance, lean upon it during times of weariness. It will support you and give you strength. As you walk upon your journey of discovery, use the staff to remove any rocks that stand in your way. Use it with a constant, steady motion to push away any obstacles. No matter how intimidating the forces which threaten to block your progress, this staff will never falter. It can never break. It is a sturdy staff worthy of you. Its strength grows the more you use it.

Allow this staff to guide you, to help you move forward against any fears that would hold you back. This staff represents your disciplined thoughts and righteous action as you walk the spiritual path.

The third gift we present to you, the gleaming sword by your side, is there should you need it. The sword represents sudden and swift action. Rarely is it used. It is only with great wisdom do you bring the sword into battle. For now it is enough to know you possess it and what it represents.

The sword is drawn from its sheath in times of great darkness. There are many uses for this sword, but most often it is used in helping others. It has great power to aid those who are struggling to find their way out of the shadows, and who seek your help as a warrior and a protector. Only those who have great wisdom will know when to use the sword. Do not be tempted to use it unwisely, but you can have a curiosity about it. It is an effective weapon of enormous energy. Do not be frightened of its image, but feel the power of it by your side and know it is there at all times.

This sword given to you is similar to the sword used in ancient Japan. It is the sword of the samurai. A responsible warrior never pulled the sword from its covering unless the intention was to draw blood. Once the sword was brought out into the open it had to be used, even if the warrior used it on himself.

This sword is the sword of righteousness spoken of in the Bible, but so misunderstood. The ego's version of this sword is based upon its own definition of strength and is used to justify the ego's anger. The true sword of righteousness is spiritual strength and power at its most forceful. It is used to battle ignorance, confusion, jealousy, and selfishness.

This sword is given not for display, not to threaten and intimidate. It cannot be used to assert your own will. Its effectiveness is equal to the wisdom you attain by using the other gifts of strength. For now keep it by your side and be patient. You will learn more of this sword as you continue your journey.

Use these symbols of spiritual strength to help you in your personal evolution. When you have learned from them and grown wise from their application, then you can use them to help others. Your own gentleness, your own perseverance and your own spiritual power will be called upon to help others overcome the obstacles hindering their growth. You can only give to others what you possess. Unless these qualities are a real part of your life, an effective source of power and strength, you cannot possibly impart that strength to those in need. Therefore, take responsibility for these gifts and use them wisely.

Impatience, undisciplined action, and recklessness will dull the sword, break the staff and tear the fan. These gifts cannot be used with anger, with thoughts of revenge, or with the intention to deceive. These symbols given to you are sacred. Guard them and make them precious in your life. Use them to discipline your mind. Use them to aid in your decisions. In times of conflict ask yourself which of these three symbols would be most appropriate? When the image is clear you will know the right action to take. You will know how much energy you should give to a particular situation.

By doing so you learn when the gentle tap of a fan would be the most effective or when the steady persistence of the staff is required. You will learn when patience is needed or when swift action and enormous energy will remedy the situation. And, when you are ready, you will begin to learn the power of the sword and its ability to destroy darkness and bring forth light.

Take these gifts into your awareness. Begin to use them. You have come a long way, but still the journey continues. Take the spiritual gifts and abilities that are your inheritance and use them in the world. Use them with wisdom. Use them with love.

# Chapter 10

## Intellect

As humanity first began to evolve into the dominant species on the planet earth, the survival mechanism of the ego began its ascendancy in mankind's awareness and the intellectual capabilities of the mind began to expand. As a physical creature humans were at a disadvantage. Other creatures of the earth were stronger, faster, more cunning, and more adaptable to changing climates. To compensate for its physical deficiencies, to insure the survival of the experiment known as mankind, the intellect evolved with an astonishing leap. With an increased intellect mankind changed the natural laws of earth.

With this shift in the ancient laws of existence, awareness rather than physical skill determined the course of earth's history. Everything on earth was affected by the emergence of a new consciousness expressed by mankind. Other creatures, especially those that dwelled alongside the habitats of early man experienced an increase in their own awareness. These creatures are what you now call "pets," the dogs, cats, birds and other domesticated animals responded to the new law and experienced an increase in their own evolution. It is by this shift in ancient law that species, which would normally fear each other, can dwell side by side and achieve a degree of communication. The intellectual development of mankind brought about a new law and many species were quick to adapt.

For all that the intellect has achieved, for all the technical advancement and its numerous means of expression, the intellect has yet to realize it's full potential. Its full capabilities are limited by the restrictions of the ego. The purpose of the intellect is to serve as a tool towards greater understandings. It was developed to process information and enhance communication and thereby increase awareness. Yet, because the ego remains in the primitive vibration of mere survival, the intellect has been focused primarily on physical reality.

The intellect is quite capable of processing information beyond the realm of the physical senses, but the human mind has been so focused on earth that certain barriers have been created which hinder further growth. The intellect will only accept information that conforms to its experiences in the physical realm. That is why man creates gods in his own image, gods who are judgmental and vengeful, gods who are gentle and forgiving. The force that is God is more than the intellect can understand. The reality of God is far too great to be captured by the minds of men. And, still there are those who claim to know God's will. There are those who continue to speak of a God subject to the whims and fantasies of the human mind.

The intellect is too limited. It cannot grasp a reality beyond physical existence. It cannot comprehend that life is more than what you experience on earth. Spiritual reality cannot be contained within the limitations of physical law.

It is not the failure of spiritual reality that cannot be measured, cannot be captured and proven by your technologies. It is your machines that are at fault. Since they are formed of physical matter they can only respond to that which is of a similar vibration, much like the intellect that has been limited to accept only that which correlates to physical laws. With increased awareness, the intellect will expand and be able to recognize and process information beyond mere physical existence.

This has happened many times in the past. An individual soul who later is acknowledged as a spiritual teacher, or a group of souls working together or independently will advance human knowledge. Consider, that many things, which your intellect is willing to accept as truth, were once beyond the comprehension of your ancestors. Your technical achievements are proof of mankind's increased awareness of physical reality and its possibilities. You have accomplished much by doing so, but you have lost much in exchange. Instinctual and intuitive sensitivities have become subordinate. Your spiritual powers are almost forgotten.

No matter how developed the intellect, regardless of how well it may have served you, realize it is within the influence of the ego because mankind has used its intellectual ability to insure the survival of the species. Like the ego it is limited and like the ego it is reluctant to venture into realms unknown. Any new experiences must be acceptable to the intellect and conform to previous experiences, that is, those experiences that the mind can understand. Of course, you are also spiritual beings and many individuals have had experiences that could not be so easily explained. These events, which defy the strictures of physical law, have frightened some people, and encouraged others. Many souls have awakened to their spiritual potential by an event beyond their comprehension.

Others, perhaps frightened by the episode, distort the event by giving it a rational explanation. Too often the intellect will grasp the event and give it a name, place it into an acceptable category, apply theories and mold it into a religion. The intellect fears what it cannot understand, fears that which defies logic. To calm its fears it must give everything a reasonable explanation, applying physical principles to the phenomena in order to understand its significance. How often the experience of a spiritual force in your life is either dismissed as imagination or minimized by the intellect.

Is it not enough to have the wonderful experience of God's light touching your life without having to limit its potential with an intellectual justification?

When such experiences occur they are for the sake of your spirit, not the mind. Joy can exist without a reason. Love can be felt as a sudden rush that brings your spirit the nourishment it seeks. You are more than an intellect, more than a mind always searching for answers.

We would like to add to the teachings of the master who spoke what you call the beatitudes. We say to you, "Blessed are they who are considered ignorant by the world, for they do not rely on books, on workshops, classes, and other outside forces to gain knowledge. Blessed are they who allow life to teach them the glory of God."

Allow every moment since you came upon this earth to be a learning experience. A book, not even such a book as you now hold in your hands, can ever express the full dimensions of life. Mere words cannot give you the understandings that can only come from living life as an adventure, going forward in faith, going forward guided by wisdom.

The intellect was meant to serve you as a tool towards higher understandings. It was never meant to dominate your thoughts and restrict your experiences. The intellect is limited; therefore, do not rely upon it to fully understand the mysteries of spiritual reality. The force of God is all around you. It flows within you. Your mind is but a small part of your experience on earth. Much of what you have struggled so hard to memorize will be forgotten once the body is laid to rest, and your spirit, enriched by its time spent on earth, moves on to another adventure.

In spirit there is no mind. There is no intellect. In spirit all things are as one. In spirit you are undivided; mind, emotions, and awareness, are all as one. Go beyond the intellectual understanding. Embrace life with all its pains and sorrow, with all its joys and all the love you are capable of expressing. The light of your spirit comes not from the mind by from the heart and it radiates all around you. Be a child of light. Trust you are a child created but God. Let not the fears and worries of the intellect deny your true existence. Discipline the mind to be at rest so that the other aspects of your being can grow stronger. Trust and have faith. Give power to your heart. It will never fail you.

We have given this message in a book so that your mind may accept the invitation to evolve. Your mind is powerful and without its acceptance of new knowledge it will limit your experiences on earth. As we have said you have come upon this planet to learn, to increase your knowledge and gain additional wisdom. You have come to strengthen your spiritual abilities and by doing so increase the evolution of your soul and the evolution of humanity. Unless the mind is willing to accept, your progress will be slow, your evolution more painful than need be as inner conflict will only diminish your power and limit your experiences on earth.

When you have finished this chapter take a moment to look around you. Tell yourself, "I have come here to learn." In the next few days, as you watch and listen to life surrounding you, tell yourself, "This is where I gather knowledge." And, in all you do, whatever tasks you must do in the world, ask yourself, "In what way can I bring light?"

## Chapter 11

# Knowledge

To live is to learn. Every experience you have on earth is a lesson. Each event in your life furthers your development as you gain knowledge, expand your awareness, enhance your abilities and learn new skills. Regardless of how your ego has judged the experiences of earthly existence, whether it has judged them to be tragic or joyful, painful or exhilarating, every moment on earth adds to the beautiful masterpiece of the soul. Everything in your life has happened for a reason. Every reason is a lesson. Every lesson brings knowledge.

Knowledge is gained by embracing life and facing with strength and courage the lessons of your existence. Do not allow the ego to entangle your feet with snares of confusion. Do not allow your fears to dampen your enthusiasm. You gain so much by being in the world. On earth there are unique lessons unavailable elsewhere. There is no other way for you to gain this knowledge than to experience fully with mind, body, and soul the lessons of your particular lifetime.

True knowledge is different than the ability to memorize or gather facts to reach a conclusion. True knowledge is more than an extensive vocabulary or expertise in a specialized field of study. Institutionalized education does not lead to true knowledge. Various degrees from universities are the glorification of the intellect, the emphasis and strengthening of only a small portion of the mind. True knowledge is so much more.

A book such as this can only guide, but cannot give to you true knowledge. It is when you begin to experience the lessons, begin to feel the truth of the words within you and make them a reality in life, then you will discover true knowledge. It is much like telling a child not to touch fire because it burns. Such a child may very well listen to you and never place finger to flame. The child will rely on your experience that fire does indeed burn. However, as often happens, the child must touch fire to truly experience the power of fire, to know the sensation of a burnt finger. A painful lesson, perhaps. A lesson that could have been avoided, perhaps. But a valuable lesson, indeed. The child has learned the nature of fire by direct experience rather than merely accepting the dictates of another.

We have given a simple example, certainly, but apply the same principle to your beliefs, the way you view the world, the way you see yourself. How much, you must ask yourself, is based upon what you have been taught? How much of your life is being limited by another person's vision of life? How much are you merely imitating the viewpoints and opinions of others? You cannot live according to other people's expectations. You cannot restrict your experiences on earth to what is acceptable to society, to your peers or to your family. Ask yourself, are the fears and ambitions, the desires and discouragements you feel, truly yours, or are they no more than the continuing legacy of your family handed down from generation to generation? Then ask yourself, can there be another way?

Consider, as well, how much your beliefs have been formed by the ego. Remember, the ego views life only in terms of the physical body and its survival. It is true that even within the narrow viewpoint of the ego, lessons can still be learned. However, know that the fears, hesitations and doubts of the ego make the learning process slow and unnecessarily painful. The ego can achieve only a shallow measure of understanding, perceiving all experiences as being either beneficial or detrimental to the body. Your *True Self* transcends such limited judgments, recognizing that great knowledge can be harvested under any and all circumstances.

Your present stage in life matters little. The extent of your education is unimportant. True knowledge comes to all who desire it regardless of social status. Often true understanding comes to those most humble and sincere and willing to learn. As the Great Teacher once said, "I thank you, Lord of heaven and of earth, for hiding these things from the learned and the clever and revealing them to mere children."

Therefore, be willing to learn and grow. Be willing to seek understanding, compassion, strength, and love throughout your lifetime on earth. Should you ever reach the point where you think you have all the answers and the great mysteries of the universe are finally within your grasp, know you are deceiving yourself. There is always more to learn, always more to experience. Every time you reach a plateau of understanding, know there is another mountain to climb. Endless are the experiences of creation and great are its mysteries.

For some this may seem exhausting. This is not so. It is the ego having the same experiences over and over again though in different forms which is tiring. It is resistance and hesitation that drag behind you like heavy chains that drain your strength. It is the debilitating fear of living life totally and experiencing the wonders of creation that undermine the power of your soul. You must give yourself permission to live. You must allow your *True Personality* and its spiritual abilities to have a more active part in your life.

True knowledge will be gained when you allow the experiences of life to reach deep within you, changing the way you see reality, altering the way you see the world. You will find that many things you thought worthwhile suddenly become meaningless and those things you thought of little value will be seen as precious. That is growth that comes from true knowledge.

You may not always be able to express this knowledge in intellectual terms. To do so is often frustrating. It is when you experience the change within, the lessening of fear and hatred and ambition and selfishness, then, and only then, is seen the power of true knowledge.

Do not fear the changes within you. Seek further growth. After all, you have not come into the world to be a stagnant pool of muddy water. You were not born to seek the illusion of a secure place in the world where you will stand perfectly still, allowing life to go on around you, safe from the turmoil, safe from the pain. You came to be swept up in life and carried along the path you've chosen, changing with each new understanding. You have come to express all the gifts you've been blessed with, to use them in the world, to refine them and strengthen them. You have come into this world to evolve.

Therefore, seek the knowledge, which has the power to transform. Such knowledge can never be forgotten because it is part of your very being. It becomes part of your existence as it changes not just your beliefs, but infuses your emotions, your spirit, even your physical body with a new energy. With this deeper, true knowledge the very air around you has a new vibration.

Dear child, dear seeker, know we can only point the way, can only introduce to you new thoughts, but it is life which will teach you. At this time we encourage you to seek those experiences, which will break the bounds of the ego and free your spiritual gifts. Seek to discover. Learn who you truly are so the light within can illuminate and dispel the darkness of ignorance. Fulfill the reason why you have come into this world. Know that we are with you as you go forth. Seek that which enlightens the soul and all of heaven rejoices.

## Chapter 12

# Wisdom

As you go forward in life you do so with wisdom. As you face new experiences, as you gather knowledge, as you take the next step in evolution, know there is wisdom guiding you. It is a powerful force that flows throughout the universe touching all of creation. It surrounds you, is within you, can never leave you.

Whereas the intellect is merely the mental ability to process information, and knowledge is something you gain through experience, wisdom is always with you. It is this great wisdom which has brought you to earth, helped you to be born, has ordered the pattern of cells to form a physical body best suited for your soul. It has guided you towards the best circumstances needed for your education. It is this great wisdom that helps bring about your evolution.

So vast and complex is this wisdom. So multi-dimensional it cannot be fully understood by the human intellect. Mere words cannot describe the force of this wisdom. We can only convey some of its attributes. We can only give you a small understanding as to the nature of this wisdom. We can present to you only some of its qualities, those you may be able to perceive.

The wisdom we speak of is boundless in its power, varied in its vibration, touching all aspects of life. It is wisdom that orders the universe, which sets planets and moons on a precise course. It is this all-prevailing wisdom in which all of creation shifts into perfect balance with the implosion of a star or the birth of a child. Nothing is outside this wisdom. It effects all of creation.

Yes, there is wisdom all around you. The ego does not understand this. It looks upon the world and sees chaos, danger, and things it cannot control, and so it denies the universal wisdom of creation. The ego trusts more in its intellect, defining wisdom as something gathered through books and years of study and the achievement of academic honors. But there was an ancient time in world history when those considered wise were men and women who experienced life totally and were able to tap into the universal wisdom, glimpsing its mysteries, understanding its powers. These ancient ones were the mystics of their time, the saints and shamans, the medicine men and healers of their people. What you call "magic" was nothing more than the ability to work in harmony with this wisdom we speak of.

There are many ways you can experience one or more levels of this wisdom. Some individuals develop their psychic abilities so as to see beyond the realm of physical matter. Others have an acute sense of intuition, sensitivity to changes in vibration, able to interpret the "feelings" surrounding a situation, an event, or a particular person. Some people dedicate themselves to the healing arts, having within themselves a knowledge that aids the physical body in correcting any energetic imbalances.

In these ways and in others, human awareness becomes cognizant of universal wisdom. The ability to do so is also within you. You first need to trust that ability within your awareness. You must first begin to believe. This book will not convince you that such wisdom exists. You must search for it yourself. You must find the wisdom within.

Therefore, we suggest the practice of what you call meditation. Develop for yourself the art of contemplation. There are many roads that lead to inner awareness. Many different forms of meditation have been cultivated in the soil of various religions and cultures. Find what is best suited for your personality. Find that which appeals to your heart, not just the mind. For now, we suggest you simply take time to sit quietly and comfortably and give consideration to the words you have read. Then close your eyes and relax. Discipline the mind away from the cares and worries of the ego.

If your mind tends to wander, give it a focus: soft music to increase relaxation, a quiet prayer, or an image of your choosing which invokes a calm state of mind. With practice and discipline you will find within you a sense of peace, a sense of unspoken knowingness. Within you is the knowledge that life is eternal. Within you is the feeling of being loved.

By calming the intellect and removing yourself from the conflicts of the ego, you can tap into the wisdom of your soul that contains the knowledge accumulated during many lifetimes on earth. You can tap into the wisdom of nature and begin to explore the wisdom of the universe. Do not doubt this. Do not allow the intellect to confuse you. Do not let the mind distract you.

If you would only, at this time, forsake the restrictions of the intellect and simply acknowledge the possibility of the existence of universal wisdom you will take a significant step in your evolution. Realize you have come into this world with the guidance of great wisdom. You did not come into this world blindfolded, stumbling along the twists and turns of earthly existence in confusion and fear. You came with eyes wide open. But, in the world of egotistical awareness, in a world where the exclusive focus is on physical reality, your insight grew dim, your psychic abilities were forgotten, your intuition suppressed by the intellect.

You have not lost the wisdom you were born with; it still remains. Realize you can begin to call upon that wisdom regardless of your education, regardless of your present situation in life, regardless of what experiences you've had in the past. All you need to do is begin to trust the ability within you to reach for this wisdom. Begin to trust the wisdom of those spiritual forces that surround you. Trust that with the power of universal wisdom you can learn what is needed to evolve, to change the patterns of your life and discover a new way of walking in the world. You can go forward with wisdom and confidence if you would only try. You do not have to earn this wisdom, though you may need to humble yourself and admit you do not have all the answers. You may need to be vulnerable and open enough to call upon wisdom greater than yourself. But for all who seek, it shall be given.

Universal wisdom does exist. It always has and it always will be. The universal wisdom we speak of is a force unlike anything the mind can comprehend, nevertheless, it is there for you. It is a force you can call upon in times of confusion, in times of despair, in times of illness, and in times of strife. Most importantly, it can be called upon in quiet rest when the mind is calm, the heart is at peace, and the needs of the soul take precedence over all else. Call upon this wisdom. Call upon this force that is stronger than the ego, wiser than the intellect, greater than any words can express.

Call upon this universal wisdom as you continue the journey of life on earth. Seek this wisdom in all situations. See how it flows through the entire universe, giving meaning to life, giving harmony to all of creation. Use this wisdom to see beyond your limitations. Begin to see and experience the force of wisdom guiding each step you take, though at times it is painful, though at times you grow weary, though you are tempted to rest upon your achievements. The force of wisdom urges you on.

# Chapter 13

▼

# Trust

Seeking wisdom takes little effort, but it does take sincere desire and it does require you to trust. It requires having the faith to reach out for a reality beyond the physical world. Therefore, take a moment at this time. Place your hand on the center of your chest and, if you like, say a prayer, one that you are fond of, a prayer you find comforting. It matters little what religion or tradition it comes from or if it is a formal prayer or your own words spoken from the heart. It may be nothing more than simply saying, "Please be with me."

Take a moment to do just that. Rest quietly and trust yourself to receive the great wisdom surrounding you. Look inward and be aware of your feelings. The trust we speak of is having faith in yourself and in the universal wisdom that flows through all of creation. It is within you though it may be hidden much like a diamond buried beneath the earth. Disappointment, awkwardness, doubt, and feelings of not being worthy of the wisdom may hide the brilliance of your faith.

You have reached a new stage in your journey, a crossroads in your path. Another decision is to be made. At this point you are being asked to trust. So far, you have been guided, encouraged, helped in ways you are not yet aware of, and even indulged to some extent. Spiritual forces have been making a great effort to prove to you that a new way of being is at hand. Know as well, we in the spiritual realm have done much within our power to lessen any interference that would deter you. The spiritual forces of universal wisdom have great power. So do you. But you must now begin to trust the spiritual power and abilities within yourself and have faith in the power of light in your life.

Have faith in yourself and trust in God, though your ego may insist that danger lies ahead, though you grow weary from the great effort needed to change your life, though you want to turn back because confusion is overwhelming. Trust you have the ability and the help of unseen forces to overcome any obstacles. As it has been said, "Blessed are they who do not see, but still believe." That is not to say that faith is blind. The trust we speak of comes from actually knowing there is more to life than what the eye can see.

Take this time to consider the disappointments of the past that will keep you from believing and experiencing spiritual reality. Understand that it was the ego trusting what you saw or what you heard in the physical world that deceived you and caused pain. This was done out of ignorance, but you did learn the truth of a situation. You gained much knowledge by experience. Yes, you learned what appears to be honest, may not be so. You may have learned that friends were not as trustworthy as you had hoped, and those who claimed to love you were influenced more by their fears than their affection. You learned by such experiences that all that glitters is not gold. Such lessons teach you to look deeper, to see beyond mere appearances.

As you search for the light of faith within you take time to consider those painful experiences of the past when you were disappointed, when you lost hope, and when you stopped trusting. Begin to realize that all those experiences, painful as they may be, were part of your education. Each experience was a lesson. Consider how your ego was hurt because things did not work out as you expected. Consider how often you trusted what you saw to be precious gold only to learn it was actually a worthless rock.

It is the ego's limited judgments of those painful situations that have led to disappointment, doubt and cynicism. It is the fear of getting hurt again which keeps you from trusting. To the ego, mistrust is a form of protection, a way to keep from being fooled again. But, such mistrust is like a dog that barks at any noise in the dark, unable to distinguish what is a threat from what is helpful.

The ego cannot comprehend the reason for such lessons. In its ignorance it becomes bitter, suspicious, and self-protective. It does not know the meaning of faith. It is reluctant to trust. For some the pain is so great they come to believe God has abandoned them. For them there is no God. There is no realm of spirit, only the harsh reality of earth as the pain of the past continues on forever. Such people have lost hope. For others, there is the egotistical belief of trusting only in the self; relying on one's own abilities to such an extreme that no one else matters. Such individuals believe that whatever is beneficial to the self is good; regardless of any pain and sorrow it may cause others. This is a false and dangerous belief, and we warn you of the potential harm done to your soul. Such a self-centered illusion is the ego at its most primitive. Does it work in the world? Yes, for some people. There is no denying that a few such individuals can even achieve wealth and fame by forsaking all else. They are not to be judged, but it is to be understood that all they have achieved in the world will someday end and they will have to face a greater reality. They will have to face the truth behind their actions on earth. Realize that those who have sought and found for themselves the rewards of selfish indulgence are not to be envied. They are merely souls who must learn their particular lessons.

The trust we speak of is greater than what the ego can offer. It is deep within you. It is spiritual wisdom that sees the harmony of the universe and knows the part you play as a spiritual force in unity with an eternal power. You must trust yourself in order to trust in the universal wisdom. You must trust your spiritual abilities. Trust in your individual wisdom. But you must also trust in the greater spiritual reality, which surrounds you and flows through you. Have faith in the universal wisdom as you gather lessons on earth. Have faith in this glorious wisdom to help you.

As you continue on your journey of evolution you will still experience times of doubt. The fears of the ego will cause you to be hesitant as you approach uncharted territory. With awareness, such times will be only momentary distractions. Each time you face your own doubts and fears, each time you resist the cynicism and ridicule of others, you strengthen your faith. Consider how often and in how many ways you have trusted others more than yourself. Because an individual has been given worldly acclaim, has gained material wealth, or a position of responsibility, you are willing to trust this one individual more than yourself.

You would rather trust the viewpoints and opinions and education of those gathered around you than to rely upon your own *True Self*. Remember, what others have come into the world to experience and learn may be quite different than the path you have chosen. Yes, there are those in the world who can offer assistance. Listen to those who will guide you to seek the power within your own spirit. Be wary, however, of those who would say the way to the Kingdom is along this particular path according to these particular methods, found only through these particular disciplines. Beware of those who have become merchants, selling their spiritual wares: ambitious, dictatorial, self-glorifying. Beware of those who would rob you of your power so they themselves can appear more powerful to the world.

Help can come to you in many ways. If you are sincere the help you need will come to you, but not always in the way you would expect. There are many Servants who walk the earth in secret. They do not work for worldly recognition. Their only reward is to do the will of universal wisdom. When they come upon a true seeker they offer an encouraging word, a helping hand, an admonishment if needed, then they are gone. They do what they can to help you find the kingdom within.

There are as well unseen forces at work in your life. Trust in them and call upon them for you are not alone. We who dictate these words do so to help, but that is only a small part of our capabilities. For every soul that seeks the light there are many of us who reach out to that soul. We do so out of love. Trust that we do what we can for the sake of your soul and no real harm will come to you. We cannot keep you from your lessons. We cannot keep away pain, if you would benefit from the experience, but we do help you in your quest to reach new understandings and a greater awareness. We guide you towards the power and glory of your own soul and the magnificence of creation. We ask you now to have faith.

Unless you begin to trust yourself, you will never find the Kingdom of Light and Power that is within you, which is your spiritual inheritance. Believe in your life. Trust the road beneath your feet. Walk forward in faith. You have the God-given ability to fulfill your destiny.

Trust who you are. Trust that you have within you what is needed to face the challenges of earthly existence. Trust there is more to you than what you see in the mirror, more to you than what others have said, more to you than what the past would indicate. If you would only trust then you will truly see. You will see with more than your eyes alone. Fears, doubt, disappointment, feelings of unworthiness limit your ability to truly see the nature of reality. They are like blinders. When you begin to trust in yourself, when you begin to have faith in God's creative force surrounding you, then you open yourself up to new experiences. These experiences will help you see the wisdom and harmony of creation and will further strengthen your faith.

When you begin to uncover the diamond of faith beneath the rubble then you will begin to discover true love. You will then have the faith to allow that power of love to flow through you. Trust awakens the power of true love, the power to have love for yourself, love for others, and a love for the beauty of God's creation.

Trust, that as an expression of God's creativity, as an expression of divine love, much has been given to you. Trust in God's power so your own *True Personality* can shine forth. Remove the chains of confusion and fear. Allow the light of faith to enter. Believe with all your heart, mind and soul, that you are guided by wisdom as you walk this earth. With this wisdom comes great strength and Divine Love.

This trust, this inner faith we speak of, is needed if you are to realize in your life all we've given you so far. All these different aspects of spiritual evolution are connected, each affects the other. Without trusting yourself and spiritual reality, you cannot attain universal wisdom. Without this wisdom you lack strength. Without strength you become fearful. Fear breeds mistrust. Therefore, do not let the disappointments of the past be carried into your future. Do not be blinded by needless suspicions. Yes, be aware of the challenges of earthly existence, but also trust you have the ability to meet those challenges. Learn to trust yourself, not with the selfishness of the ego, but as a spiritual being, a force of light which can conquer the darkness.

# Chapter 14

▼

# Forgiveness

As you begin to seek inner faith and come to trust yourself and your abilities, you must first cross a small bridge. We call this the "bridge of forgiveness." At this point in your journey you make the emotional decision to evolve. You have come this far by making the intellectual decision to move forward, but now you must make the emotional decision. Now you must step upon this bridge of forgiveness so as not to carry the past into the future.

Put your hand on your heart, take a deep breath and relax. See yourself standing at the foot of a bridge. Stand there quietly. Take a brief moment to look back. See the past you leave behind. See the old disappointments and ancient sorrows as vague shadows far in the distance. You do this so you may release them. The way to let them go is to forgive.

Take another deep breath. Calm yourself. Even though this is a small bridge it can be a difficult one to cross. Remember, you have received three symbols of strength—the fan, the staff, and the sword. You may need all three to cross this bridge.

As you start across the bridge you will begin to call forth all those in the past and those presently in your life who have hurt you. Allow into your awareness the faces of those who have caused you pain. Some people will appear suddenly before you, people you have almost forgotten, and people you remember all too well. With each face, each name and each memory of pain, begin to forgive.

Recall the classmates and childhood friends who laughed at you and forgive them. Recall when your parents acted unwisely, or were insensitive and forgive them. Recall employers who may have been unfair or caused you stress. Forgive them. Now is the time to forgive those who died and left you alone.

Allow to come into your mind all those you loved but who rejected you, not because of who you are, but because they could not see, could not accept, because they were frightened. Begin now to forgive them. Bring into mind the lovers in your life, even if they were a part of your life for only a brief moment. Recall the pain, the difficulties, the misunderstandings, and their final departure. Remember how it felt and begin to forgive.

Now is the time to forgive all those who hated you, who despised and ridiculed you, those who considered themselves to be your enemy. Forgive all enemies.

Let their faces come to mind. Let the incidents of the past be remembered no matter how painful, no matter how much you would rather forget. Allow the images and feelings to arise so you can release them with forgiveness.

Realize you have kept these memories and their remnant pain within you. You have held on to them. You may have thought you had forgotten, that you shrugged them off and turned your back against them, however, realize that each experience is held within your memory and still effects how you walk in the world. You have not yet released the pain through forgiveness. You have not looked upon each experience with wisdom and love and strength.

Realize the ego uses these memories to remember what is painful and to keep you guarded against future pain. This keeps you from moving forward. Unless you forgive and release the pain it will always be a part of you like a heavy chain dragging behind you, clanking loudly and slowing your evolution. Release this chain that binds you.

As you walk across this bridge and encounter the faces of pain and sorrow you may feel once again the anger, feel once again the heartache of rejection and loneliness. Even the memory of physical pain could be felt anew and cause you to retreat in fear. Realize those old feelings stand in your way of truly forgiving. When this happens you must use the symbols of strength given to you. Use your inner strength to cross this bridge, forgiving those who would stand in your way, determined to go beyond the pain of the past.

With some memories you may need only the fan to gently forgive and move on. You may see clearly and with amusement the misunderstandings that occurred so long ago. With other memories the images may seem quite solid, quite real as you re-experience the pain. In such a case you may feel great reluctance to forgive. You may feel only anger towards the person who caused you such harm. It is then you must take the staff of perseverance and walk steadily past the offender with the simple words, "I forgive you."

And in those relationships that were especially close to you, in those experiences in which the pain is too deep and the heartache is too devastating, great strength will be needed. When you resist having to look at the experience again and you fear the anguish and torment of the open wound use the sword to cut away the fear, to destroy the weakness, and dispel the darkness of that memory. Use the sword to cut away the chains of that memory that darken your life and use the power of forgiveness to end your suffering.

Yes, there are those people you would cherish hating, those you say could never be forgiven because the hurt is too deep, the damage too great. Begin to understand that your anger and hate, your fear and pain keep you bound to the situation and the people involved. By holding on to such feelings you keep those people in your life, connected to them on an emotional level. Even though the ones who hurt you may be long gone, even dead, you remain connected to them by your feelings. They are still with you. They are still tormenting you. With forgiveness you let them go.

As you cross the bridge and face those who hurt you be aware of your own feelings towards them. If you ask yourself why forgive them; why forgive those who died and left you alone; why forgive those who rejected you; why forgive those who were so cruel? Simply say to yourself, "They did not know what they were doing."

If anyone of them had truly known there was another way of being in the world they would not have acted according to the fear and desperation of their egos. Had they known otherwise, they would not have allowed their own fear and anger and hate to blind them. How could they act from love and goodness when they did not know such power? They did not know there could be another way. Their actions towards you were according to their limited understanding. Yes, there are those in the world so lost in darkness, so ruled by their own selfishness, so much a part of what you call evil, that their actions seem cruel beyond imagination. Forgive them so you do not fear them. Forgive those who have lost their souls. They did not know what they were doing.

Forgiveness may not heal all the pain for some people. It is to their benefit that some pain remains during their journey on earth. It may be difficult to understand how a painful experience can actually be a blessing. Many lives are altered by a single, traumatic event that forced their souls to take a new direction in life. Many readers hold this book because sorrow and confusion has led them to seek answers, to seek new understandings and seek healing for the pain in their lives. Though forgiveness may not remove all the pain, it will remove the fear.

As fear is released with each step along the bridge of forgiveness you will gain strength and perhaps some understanding as to why certain events have occurred in your life. Even if you do not fully understand, even if you find it hard to feel true forgiveness, nevertheless, continue to walk, continue to say to all you meet, "I forgive you. Go in peace." After all, you can never know true forgiveness unless you have someone to forgive. And, when you begin to forgive others, you can then begin to forgive yourself.

Halfway across the bridge stop for a moment and look inward, stand alone and seek within yourself the sadness, the shame, and the guilt of your own past mistakes. With the power of forgiveness you can do so with clarity and courage. You must look at your own past and begin to forgive yourself. You cannot step off this bridge until you have learned to forgive yourself with the same love and wisdom and strength you have given to others. You must call to mind what should be considered not sins or flaws, but simply errors in judgment. Recall the times you acted unwisely, and forgive yourself. Realize that through ignorance and pain, you have hurt other people. You, too, were blind to those who were in need of your love. Forgive yourself. You, too, rejected those who may have been seeking your understanding and compassion. Forgive yourself because you were limited by the ego.

You must take responsibility for your actions in the world. You must accept the consequences. True forgiveness is to acknowledge the errors of the past, acknowledge what was done out of ignorance and to move forward in another direction. The errors were part of learning. There is no need to repeat what you have already learned. To forgive yourself is to overcome the snares of the past so errors will not be repeated. Forgiveness heals the past so the blindness, the fear, the resentments of the ego has no hold upon you.

Forgiveness is a power. It is a force that cleanses, heals, and transforms. The ego will have you believe that to forgive is to be weak. It interprets forgiveness to mean condoning an action, acquiescing to the pain, and forgetting what happened. Forgive and forget are two different words. You cannot forget the experience. That would be foolish. The experience, though painful, has made you wiser. If you would cleanse yourself of bitterness and hate, it will be easier to see the wisdom you have gained.

The ego, however, will hold on to anger, hate, sorrow, and loneliness as a shield to protect you from further pain. The ego sees itself as protecting you, but it just keeps you limited and entrapped within the darkness of ignorance. All that has happened in your life did so for a reason, though you may not always understand why.

Forgiveness is the key that unlocks the prison of the past. Don't linger trying to understand why you should leave behind the limitations that bind you. Use the power within you, use the force of your spirit to unlock the door and forgive. It is the way of the spirit, the force of your *True Personality* that can replace hate with love, exchange weakness for strength, and bring the light of wisdom to conquer the blindness of ignorance. It does so with forgiveness.

If you are willing to forgive all those who have hurt you then you have made the emotional decision to evolve. Let the past remain in the past. Realize those people are gone. Realize they have no power over you. Understand that those experiences are ancient memories and will not happen again except in your mind, if you allow it to be so. It is only with the power of forgiveness that you leave behind the pain and sorrow.

The amount of pain you feel during this part of your journey, the intense feelings of resentment and revenge that arise as you cross this bridge, are in direct correlation to the amount of resistance you have towards forgiving. If you are hesitant you will cross the bridge slowly and increase the time spent reliving the hate, the hurt and the disappointments. You can cross this bridge with sure and steady steps if you allow yourself to feel the power of forgiveness.

As you reach the part of the bridge where you begin to forgive yourself you may be hampered by feelings of shame and guilt. Do not allow such feelings to stop you. You may also feel the opposite and struggle for justification through self-pity. Do not allow such self-defense to blind you.

Feel the shame, feel the guilt, feel the self-pity, if you must, then let such feelings go and seek instead the feeling of forgiveness.

Do not be afraid to look with wisdom, strength, and gentle kindness at how you have lived your life. The errors you made were simply because you did not know any better. Had you known otherwise, you would have acted otherwise. You did not have the experience to teach you that there is another way of being in the world.

The world you came into, the people in your life, the experiences you had were all within the limitations of the ego. So were you. This is no longer necessary. Let this experience of forgiveness be the first of many experiences to teach you that a new way can exist. You can feel more than what has been felt in the past. You can be more than what you thought yourself to be. Wisdom is yours. Strength is within you. Love awaits. Put down the shield of self-protection and raise the banner of forgiveness. Crossing this bridge is a battle. It may be difficult for some readers. For others it will go quite easily. A few might think they have crossed the bridge only to find they have fooled themselves. Their journey will take them back to the bridge so once again they have the chance to forgive. You may have to cross this bridge many times, each time strengthening your resolve to battle ignorance with forgiveness.

Only you will know if you have acquired the full force of forgiveness. The power of forgiveness is not a power of the mind. Forgiveness is a power and energy that comes from the heart. You will know it by feeling it. You will feel its power as it heals your emotions. Do not hesitate to open your heart and forgive the past, forgive yourself and move in a new direction.

On the other side of the bridge you enter the realm where you find the true meaning of compassion. The concept of compassion has been so misunderstood. The ego reduces compassion to pity. The full realization of compassion is limited to feeling sorry for someone, feeling sorry for yourself. The ego's judgments limit understanding and sorrow is felt for any experience it defines as bad, that is, harmful to the ego. It looks upon such experiences with pity rather than true compassion and spiritual understanding.

Compassion is a jewel. Pity is a rock. Understand the difference. In the past you have used the rock of pity against yourself and against others. Yes, you cause more harm than good when you use that rock. You hurt others. You hurt yourself whenever pity is used. Whenever you use pity the limited judgments of the ego are reinforced.

Pity grows from the ego's sense of helplessness in a situation. You try shedding tears as if that would change it. You try throwing money at the problem, as if that would change it. You may spend great lengths of time using the intellect to analyze the cause of the problem, as if that would change it. Still, there is suffering. Still, there is poverty. The earth in its wisdom adjusts itself and you call the resulting floods, earthquakes, and windstorms a pitiful tragedy. You feel pity for those who suffer, as you would feel pity for yourself under the same circumstances.

Pity is a noose you put around your neck as you await circumstances to come along and kick the chair out from under your feet. Pity is suicide. You are killing yourself mentally and emotionally by feeling sorry for yourself. Realize that pity keeps you trapped. It is a cage also for those you feel sorry for as you reinforce and project upon them your own fears and sorrow. When you are trapped in pity you forget your inner strength. You lose trust and faith. You become deaf and blind to the force of God available to you.

If in your heart you feel the need to alleviate the suffering you see in the world then get up and do so, but not with pity. Realize that pity changes nothing. Go forth with strength, wisdom, and true compassion, and then you will have an effect in the world. Pity cripples, compassion strengthens.

You will need your strength to escape the trap of pity. Strength is needed so you can lift your feet and continue on with life. If you are willing to let go of the ego's pity you will soon discover true compassion. Therefore, put down the rock and pick up the jewel. Seek a greater understanding than what the ego offers.

We warn you against the limits of pity so you do not carry it any further. You leave it behind. As you cross the bridge of forgiveness you looked upon the experiences of your life. Once you reach the other side you begin to look upon the circumstances affecting the world, affecting the lives of those around you, and still playing a part in your own education. You will learn to look with compassion.

With true compassion you will be guided towards a greater understanding and a more expanded awareness as to the nature of both physical and spiritual reality. Compassion will lift you to a higher level of consciousness. It will keep you from relying on the limited judgments of the ego.

Compassion is a magical tool. It is there for you, for your journey on earth, for your soul's evolution. You will know you possess the jewel when you experience it working in your life. You will not have to think about it, though you may have to remind yourself in the beginning to put away pity and learn to see things in a different way, to look deeper than what is apparent, to see beyond the limited judgments of the ego. Compassion is insight. It is a part of your human consciousness that needs to be awakened by developing your spiritual abilities.

We will try to describe the nature of true compassion so as to point you in its direction, but understand we can only show a glimmer of its full illumination. We will try to impart as much as possible about compassion so you may see it shining in the darkness. But, it is up to you to seek it and make it your own. Only when you possess compassion will you truly understand its abilities. Though you may struggle and search for it, know that compassion is close at hand. Know it is yours.

In order to find the jewel we speak of, you must lift yourself out of the quicksand of hate, out of the darkness of anger, out of the shackles of pain and fear. You must throw off the yoke of pity. With the power of forgiveness, with the power of your heart and the wisdom of your soul, the gleaming jewel is within your reach.

# Chapter 15

▼

# Compassion

You have come to earth so you may learn, so you may grow and evolve. So has everyone else. Realize this and you will have compassion.

Many are the opportunities to learn, some are joyful, and some are harsh. Even painful experiences have value. Realize this and you will have compassion.

In your own life there has been hardship. There has been pain. In the world around you there is so much tragedy, so much suffering, so much heartbreak, and loneliness. We have asked you to forgive so you may be free from the despair, the pity, the anger and the fear, which is so much a part of your world. But we ask you to remember the pain, remember how it felt, remember so you do not do to others what has been done to you. Remember, so you do not add to the suffering. Remember, so you can understand the pain of others. That is compassion.

Without having experienced the pain and sorrow of earthly existence you would lack wisdom. It is by experiencing for yourself that you come to know the more difficult aspects of earthly existence. What you must realize is the pain you felt is the same pain felt throughout the world. You are not alone in your suffering. With this understanding you increase your sensitivity, your compassion, your desire to bring light into your life and into the life of others.

In the past, your ego has dealt with pain by building a wall of protection, a barrier of anger and despair. For some, it is the shield of self-pity, the mournful cry of pain internalized. For others the pain is externalized into violence, lashing out at others in revenge for a hurt that never heals. Others descend into loneliness and separation, keeping apart and hiding their hearts so as not to be hurt again. And for some there is the never—ending quest to numb the pain, to indulge in physical sensations through alcohol, drugs, food, mental distractions, and sexual obsessions.

And so you are asked to forgive and have compassion towards those who have hurt you. You do it not for their sake, but for your own evolution. With forgiveness you remove from yourself the ego's reactions to the pain. With forgiveness you can then see the situation with a better understanding. Compassion brings you that understanding. With compassion you are able to look at a situation with wisdom, with strength and, with love. Seek not revenge. Seek understanding. Seek not to protect yourself, but to free yourself of ancient fears. Seek not a life without challenge. Seek strength and courage.

Therefore, have compassion for those who have hurt you. See how what was done to you was done out of ignorance. Have compassion towards those who lash out in anger. Know they are in pain. Have compassion for the addict, the criminal, the lost and forgotten ones, for their burden of sorrows are many and the suffering they face is great. Have compassion for all you meet; rich or poor, athletic or lame, friend or enemy, regardless of race, regardless of religion, regardless of the differences you see. All are struggling to learn. All have the light of God within them. Have compassion, but know as well, that there is another way to be in the world for you and for them.

Understand, however, that some souls must live a life of selfishness, a life of anger and violence, a life of addiction. It is the way the soul will learn. It is not yet their time to evolve. Have compassion for them, forgive, but do not condone. Instead, speak of another way. Plant seeds of mercy and love; speak of a greater way to be in the world. Your words of wisdom can never be wasted. What does not take root in this lifetime, may take root in the next. Understand this and you will have compassion.

Look beyond the limits of time to that which is eternal and compassion is yours. Look beyond the superficial and compassion will give you insight. Compassion cannot be limited. Unlike pity, compassion is not given to a few unfortunates. Compassion is all embracing. Compassion is the awakening of true love. It goes beyond the individual self and reaches beyond personal experiences to achieve a greater understanding.

Compassion knows another's pain. It knows the sorrow others feel. It knows loneliness. It knows rejection. It knows the pain of physical suffering. Compassion embraces this and more. Joy, laughter, peace; all are felt with compassion.

The jewel of compassion has the ability to enlighten the mind, enrich the heart, and guide your actions in the world. A compassionate mind has the ability to see beyond the illusion of separation. It sees beyond differences and sees instead God's creative force flowing throughout all of creation. The compassionate heart continues to love, continues to burn brightly, while still feeling the piercing thorns of pain and suffering.

Compassionate action is based on a single heart-felt decision. Ask yourself, will you add to the suffering in this world, will you make things worse, or will you bring light and love into the world? Compassion knows what to do. Compassion will decide. Compassion sees beyond the needs of the ego, sees the needs of the world and acts accordingly.

That is not to say, dear seeker of truth, dear compassionate one, that all you do will be welcomed in the world. Courage will be needed. You will need strength to be compassionate. It takes strength to say what the world does not want to hear. Compassion speaks so that foolishness is silenced.

Compassion acts without fear of judgment. Compassion defies the laws of government when those laws defy God. You will need strength and courage and wisdom, but most of all you will need love. Much love will be needed, love for creation, love for all.

You will need love to resist falling into judgment. Love will overcome revulsion and pity. Without love you will become nothing more than a self-righteous crusader. Remember, you are not marching off to war determined to correct what you have judged to be right and condemning those you think are wrong. Compassion does not judge.

Compassion looks beyond the superficial and sees the force of God within another human being, sees the same force of God within yourself, know it is one and the same. Compassion sees the golden thread of God weaving all of creation together and what it sees it loves. With the power of compassion you transcend the struggles of survival in this world. Your consciousness extends beyond mere physical existence and perceives the greater spiritual reality of life.

With the jewel of compassion in your possession you begin to see a greater truth. You realize that whether Buddhist, Christian, Jewish, Moslem, on whatever path an individual finds himself or herself, all share in the deep desire to seek something greater in life. All are attempting to take that next step which will lead to new understandings, new experiences, and a new way to walk in the world. The judgments of the ego see only the differences, only those things that separates, only that which it condemns as inferior. Such is the limitations of self-righteousness.

Use your compassionate mind to realize that many paths lead to the top of the mountain. There is no exclusive path for all. The force you call God is known by many names and all should be respected but no single name can capture its immense force. No single dogma will convey its majesty. From each spiritual path there is much to learn, but focus on where you are walking rather than where others may be going. Follow your path of evolution faithfully, not because it is the only way, or the superior way, but because it is the way you will best learn.

Though compassionate, you will still have your own preferences, your own personal way of being in the world based upon your particular gifts and the lessons you wish to learn while on earth. You have your path to follow as others have their own journey. Certainly you may go on preferring vanilla ice cream if you like, but it is the ego that would judge those who choose chocolate as wrong. Certainly you will dress in a way which is comfortable and suits you, but it the ego which insists all others wear the same fashion. Silly examples, yes, but see how this same judgment is used in other areas of your life. See where you condemn those who are different. See how you hold preconceived images based on the ego's judgments.

Saint or sinner, two different paths, still God is within both. Beggar or businessman, two different experiences, still each is a part of creation, each worthy of your compassion. The ego sees only with its eyes. The Compassionate one sees with the heart.

Know that personal evolution is more than the gathering of facts. It is more than extending the mind's knowledge. Evolution alters your personal energy, rising above the slower vibrations of ego to the higher vibration of the divine. Evolution alters how you think, how you feel, and how you walk in the world.

It will take effort on your part. It will take discipline and it will take patience. So, take the time needed to grow. Heal your pain with forgiveness. Walk in the world with love. Find the forgotten light within you, and then bring what you have learned into the world. That is compassion.

# Chapter 16

▼

# A Gift For Your Soul

The Christ has said, "Judge not, lest ye be judged."

The Christ has said, "As you would judge others, so shall you be judged." This judgment comes not from God, but from yourself. The condemnation, the judgments, and the criticisms you project onto the world will become your reality. It is the judgments you have made about life which create your experiences on earth.

The ego externalizes its fears into the world. It projects its opinions and its judgments through thought forms. Every thought has a power. When your emotions are in agreement with your thoughts the power increases. Your mental, emotional, and physical energies create your life. If an individual thinks he or she is poor then the ego will create a reality of poverty. Even in the midst of abundance, the individual remains in a state of emotional and mental poverty and his or her actions will reflect that inner struggle.

When an individual is fearful, thinking and feeling him or her to be powerless, the ego will project an image of a frightening world. If an individual feels isolated and alone, he or she will create an environment of isolation. His or her thoughts and actions will keep others away.

Your thoughts and emotional energies have a magnetic pull, attracting people and events of similar vibration. Fear will attract fearful experiences. Poverty, which is an obsession for material things the ego deems worthwhile, will create a reality of despair and dissatisfaction. Loneliness creates a barrier of isolation, a self-consciousness in which all energy is turned inward.

These judgments are a trap. They are internal decisions you have made which continue to influence your reality. When you judge yourself, when you judge others, when you judge the world, you create for yourself a reality based on those judgments. You condemn yourself to the limitations of the ego. Few people are able to realize this phenomenon of creativity. Few are able to release themselves from the chains of their own opinions.

To do so we offer you the jewel of compassion. You must first give yourself this gift before you can give it to others. Only when you feel compassion for yourself will you feel compassion for the world around you. Only when you let go of the judgments you've made against yourself will you come to know true compassion. With this jewel you free yourself from the bounds of the limited ego. With this gift you evolve.

Your spiritual evolution begins when you see beyond the narrow viewpoint of the ego. You see beyond its definitions of what is right and what is wrong, what is worthwhile and what is deemed worthless. With the jewel of compassion there is nothing that is ugly and there is nothing that is beautiful. There is no rich. There is no poor. You no longer judge yourself and others according to the dictates of the ego. You see yourself as a spiritual being, an eternal force evolving and transforming within the masterpiece of God's creation.

Though you may not have material abundance you are still worthy of God's love. Though you may be alone, still there is much for you to share. Though you may now be afraid, still you have power and strength. Begin to accept who you truly are in this world. Accept the spiritual abilities that aid in your evolution. You must accept as well the mistakes of the past. By these errors you have learned. Forgive yourself for acting out of ignorance. Accept the wisdom those experiences have given you. Allow the light of Divine Love to touch you.

You have been given symbols of strength. Use all three, if need be, to conquer the judgments of the ego. Use your strength to vanquish your limited criticisms of yourself and others. Use your strength to vanquish any guilt you may have from past actions in the world.

Guilt keeps you from finding the jewel of self-compassion. It holds you in the past. It strengthens the judgments of the ego. It encourages the false identity you may have of yourself. Heal the past with compassion. On this spiritual path there will be times you will have to review your history as memories emerge, old feelings are remembered, and what was once forgotten is found again. That which the ego had once justified as righteous, that which the ego has denied, that which the ego holds precious will be seen with new understanding.

When mistakes of the past arise in your consciousness there is often denial as the ego seeks to protect itself and its actions. The ego will defend its actions, find justification or cast the blame on an outside force. When denial fails, as it must at some point, there are often feelings of shame, self-pity, and guilt.

Again, the ego is judging. The ego is punishing itself for having made a mistake. If wisdom has been gained and correction of action taken, then there is no need for guilt. If you feel the need to make restitution, then do so. If you feel the need to apologize then do so. But, it is not enough to correct an unwise action outwardly. You must also make the adjustments within yourself. Guilt and shame may serve as a reminder that certain actions are detrimental, but they also keep you bound to the past. Compassion heals the pain of the past.

True compassion changes the emotional and mental attachments to previous experiences. With compassion you are able to alter the vibrations of those experiences, past and present, which continue to influence your life and continue to create your reality. Compassion brings light into a situation, seeing an event with strength, wisdom, and with love. With spiritual insight you are able to see the truth of a situation. Perhaps you may not always understand the deep wisdom of a certain event in your life, but you can change its effect on your mental and emotional energies. The ego retains the pain of the past through its judgments.

For instance, a painful experience will continue its influence throughout an individual's life, influencing how that individual sees the world and how he or she will act in accordance to the ego's judgments of that event. Even when a particular experience may be consciously forgotten it will still exert an influence on a personality. The ego reacts to the past, but cannot heal it.

With compassion you move beyond the limited and slower vibrations of the ego. You move beyond the ego's judgments. When you feel compassion within you a change occurs, subtle at first but increasingly more powerful with practice. Your spiritual energy is strengthened. Your vibration is heightened. Within you and around you there is an intensity as your energy becomes brighter, more colorful, and more powerful. What you think of yourself will change and this effects how you walk in the world. Without the burdensome lower vibrations of the ego's judgments you will begin to experience a new reality. That is the gift you give to yourself.

When you grasp the jewel of compassion the shadows of the past can no longer frighten you. Guilt and sorrow can no longer possess you. False judgments will no longer blind you. We must tell you, however, that this beautiful jewel is difficult to obtain. You must be sure you are strong enough to find it. You must desire to have it no matter what the cost. The ego holds on to its judgments as a means of self-protection. You must have courage to let go of your judgments. You will need strength and power, as there is much to be sacrificed in order to obtain the jewel.

The biggest sacrifice to be made is the image you have of yourself. Compassion will change you. But, after all, evolution is change. As we have said, you have not come into this world to stand still. You have come to learn and to grow. You are on earth to evolve. Some people have become too comfortable with the slower vibration of the ego and its slower growth. For those who choose the spiritual path of evolution changes will often occur quite suddenly in unusual and wonderful ways. Therefore, do not be surprised when there are times you do not recognize yourself. It is your self-image evolving.

Much of your present personality was formed by the ego's judgments of experiences during your present lifetime. As you look at those events with compassion your identity will also be transformed. Beliefs that were once held so dear, likes and dislikes so freely expressed, preferences even for small inconsequential things may suddenly become meaningless. Be forewarned, the ego without its judgments feels vulnerable and it will struggle for dominance. It feels protected by its ability to judge, even when those judgments are false and deceptive.

As the inner transformation from judgment to compassion begins you will at times feel vulnerable, unsure of yourself, perhaps confused and even frightened. Take your time and be patient. Do not expect instant changes to occur. All you need to do is discipline yourself to seek understanding; looking upon a situation with increased awareness, knowing that every event has a meaning, every experience is a lesson. Compassion will guide you towards a greater awareness once the veil of the ego's judgments is brushed aside.

You can give this gift to yourself. Only you and no one else are capable of giving such a precious jewel to call your own. Do not waste time waiting patiently for someone to come into your life and pat you on the head saying everything will be all right. Don't sit alone in your room waiting for another person to chase away the fears and present you with love. And, there is no point in waiting for the rest of the world to evolve before you'll agree to do so. What you seek is within you. The gift of compassion is there at hand, but it is you who must reach out for it.

You will have help, of course. You always have help. But to give you such a gift without making an effort only weakens the recipient and darkens the jewel. You will have to make an effort to leave behind your limited judgments. It will take great effort, but you have the strength and the power. And, you have our help. Always remember, we are with you.

Sit quietly for a while and know we are near. Sit quietly and be at peace. Place your hand on the center of your chest and breath deeply. Nothing else matters for this moment. Focus only on yourself. In this moment there is no past and there are no thoughts of the future. Awaken your heart. Feel compassion for yourself. Feel the love we bring you. No matter what mistakes have been made, no matter what crimes committed, no matter what sins oppress you, we give you our love. We give it freely.

We give you this love so you may feel compassion for yourself. The jewel of compassion is closer than you know. The door that has hidden this jewel has now been opened. You opened that door by forgiving those around you and by forgiving yourself. Forgiveness has opened the door. With patience and discipline you will find the jewel.

Use what you have learned so far. Seek greater understanding in all you see and experience. Move past the old shadows that darken your light. Move past the judgments that slow your evolution. Look upon yourself with love and compassion. For the sake of your spirit open your heart.

# Chapter 17

▼

# A Reminder

Remember you were created in the image of God. By that we mean to say that within you is a force of God, an eternal, sacred energy that has brought you into existence and continues to flow through you. One way that force manifests itself through you is in the form of creativity. You are a created entity and you are a creative force in the universe.

Like it or not your participation brought about the world you see around you. You are not a victim of what surrounds you. You are not a prisoner of time and space. You are not a victim of forces greater than your own power. You have not come onto earth to be a lamb led to slaughter.

You are in this world because you created it. You have the right to do with this world whatever you please. You have the choice of using wisdom or ignorance. You have the choice of cherishing your creation or abusing it, believing that what happens to earth will have no effect upon you. You have the choice of believing yourself separate from the creative force of God, thinking this has no effect on you. Or, you have the choice of taking the next step in evolution and developing your inherent abilities to see beyond the physical realm, to understand deeper than the ego can perceive, to feel within you the power of creativity.

It is what you choose in life that will create your reality. No matter what you choose, you cannot deny that you are creating your life. You have created it so far through the thought patterns of the ego. That is one way. What others call the reality of human existence is no more than the ego expressing itself. It is a primitive way and has its limitations, but if you wish to continue repeating the old way, that is your choice.

If, however, you seek the next step in your development you must begin to learn new thought patterns and be willing to accept new experiences in order to discover who you truly are, in order to express your *True Personality* and it's wonderful abilities.

Until this moment you have been creating your life in a simple way. The colors you used were dark. The form was vague. It lacked harmony. It lacked richness in feeling. Its full beauty was never realized. You settled for less. It was all you knew. It was how you've been taught. It is the way of the world that encompasses you.

Put aside the ways of the ego and you will find within yourself a greater creativity. The colors in your life will be brighter. The form will be strong, a creation of harmony and love. Not all, but still many people will see this force of creativity flowing through you. Not all will understand. When you create with such beauty and light there will be no need to hide it. You allow such beauty to shine forth and be seen. When you create with this newfound sense of power there will be no fear or hesitation in allowing it to be seen. You cannot help but share this energy with those who will accept it.

It matters little if you cannot draw a simple line. It does not matter if you never painted or played a musical instrument or even cared about art in any of its forms. That is not the creativity of which we speak.

You are the paintbrush. You are the musical instrument. You are the sculptor's chisel. Life is the canvas. Life is the symphony. Life is the beautiful stone that you carve to discover the masterpiece contained within.

Remember this. Remain aware of your potential. Stay mindful of how creative you can be.

We tell you this so you may remove from your consciousness any of the ego's concepts of being a victim. We remind you of your power so you will walk in the world as a creative force. Put away the judgments of the ego that will have you believe you are either less than other people or arrogantly think you are superior.

Be mindful of your thoughts. Be aware of the words you speak. Put away from you limitations that have been imposed upon you. Never say, "It's not possible to be anything else." Do not allow your ego to claim, "I can't do it." Cleanse your thinking of such statements as, "It's not my fault," or "There is nothing I can do." Such words are the limitations of the ego. They are lies. They are the words of a victim. They will hinder your development. They will keep you attached to the limited image you have of yourself.

Be mindful that all experiences in the physical world have value. You have come to learn certain lessons. Some people have chosen poverty to learn appreciation for those things greater than material goods. Many have come into the world with bodies that are deformed to learn how unimportant the physical form is to their lives. Many souls come into the world only to die at a young age for different reasons, some to teach by their sacrifice, some to learn a specific lesson then depart. Everything happens for a reason.

The ego in fear and limited judgment does not understand the wisdom of such lessons. It does not understand that even the most painful lessons are essential for the evolutionary development of individuals. The ego in ignorance points a condemning finger and cries, "There is no God." The ego, moved by pity, cries, "Victim." The ego sees life only between the stages of birth and death. It sees the world as a threatening realm where one is either aggressor or prey. As we have said, the ego does not acknowledge its personal participation in creating the world.

We tell you there is more to life than can be imagined, more than the human mind can understand. Behind the dark colors that the ego has shown to you lies a great light, a beautiful light. That light is you. Behind the vague and misunderstood form of physical reality there is an eternal reality. Behind the self-image adopted by your ego there lies your *True Self*.

Seek what is beyond ignorance and you will find wisdom. Beyond fear there is faith. Beyond the pain and frustration of feeling separate there is true harmony. Beyond the anger and ambition, beyond self-protection and greed, there is love.

With the eyes of the ego you will never see the beauty of life. The ego is too limited and what it sees is too dim, too far in the distance. The ego seeks outside itself and places the answers to your questions beyond reach. Without the ego you may discover you knew some of the answers all along and with newfound courage could seek the answers you don't yet know.

Therefore, be open to new experiences. You must feel your spiritual power working in the world. You must have the experience of it so you will know of its reality. When you get even a glimpse of your true nature, embrace it, give it strength, believe in it and put it into action. With the wisdom of your *True Personality* you will find the tools needed to create a new life. You will see yourself in a new way. The way you see the others will change. The earth upon which you walk will have a greater dimension as you re-define how you look at reality. Through the power of your *True Personality* you will bring light into the world.

All it takes is willingness. It is your own true desire that will conquer the fears, the doubts, the hesitations, and the meaningless ambitions of the ego. We remind you of all this for you now possess the tools needed: the symbols of inner strength, the healing of pain through forgiveness, and the power of your decisions. We remind you of your own true and eternal self so the desire within you can be encouraged.

Be willing. Use what we have presented to you, even if some doubt remains, even if fear intrudes. In time you will be stronger than your fears.

In time you will move beyond your doubts. You will realize doubt and fear do not serve you. They are the creations of the ego. Why hold on to them?

As you begin to experience your *True Personality* you begin to create with a rainbow of colors. You create with a beauty and joy you have never known before. You will begin living as a masterpiece of Divine Creativity, in the image of God, created in beauty and in love. And you will go forth creating with beauty and love—creating your life now and forever.

# Chapter 18

## Discipline and Patience

The ego will tell you to *Beware*. This implies danger. This is a constant warning of an outside threat. The ego implies you are powerless. The *True Personality*, however, will tell you simply to *Be Aware*. It is more than just a matter of one letter that makes the difference between the two.

The *True Personality* favors awareness whereas the ego favors protection. The *True Personality* will tell you that it is awareness that is your real protection. Simply being aware is all you need to continue on your journey.

It sounds simple. It can be simple. But your mind keeps you so busy, so distracted that simple awareness seems out of reach. It is not. From this moment on, in all that you do, remind yourself to *Be Aware*. The first thing you must keep in your awareness is that you have not come very far from the thought patterns of the ego. Though you have read our message so far you are still within the ego. You have had glimpses of what is spiritual and you have experienced a new awakening to some degree, but you are still very much in ego. Do not judge yourself for this. Understand that the entire world is based on ego assumptions. The human structures around you, the organizations, the individuals in your life are all within the limitations of the ego. At this present time in human development the ego is still the ruling force.

Be aware, as well, that you have spent many years cultivating your ego, giving it strength, giving it your trust. You have relied upon your ego to challenges of earthly existence. It takes effort to evolve.

But with patience and discipline you will move forward. With true desire you will leave the past behind. We bring this into your awareness because you have reached the stage where the ego becomes subtle in its influence. The ego will have you believe that certain actions are spiritual when they are not. The ego will again use its limited judgments to have you believe you have advanced further than you have, or convince you that little progress has been made. Yes, you have accomplished much, but there is more.

Do not be alarmed and do not judge yourself should this occur. Learn from it. Experience it. Be aware of the subtleties of the ego. When you struggle against the ego's influence, when it rises up in anger, in lust, in desperation and fear, remember the tools you have received.

Use your inner strength. Use the symbols we have given so you can find your inner power. Say a prayer you have found that is comforting. Say it with sincerity or the words will be meaningless. Say the sacred words with a true desire in your heart. By focusing your mind on the spiritual you will regain your balance. This will help you move forward.

This, of course, takes discipline. Be aware, however, that discipline cannot replace true desire. Just going through the motions will be of little help. Discipline does not mean performing a certain action as a routine. Without desire to evolve the practice of discipline becomes only a meaningless habit. True, powerful discipline is an extension of your inner yearning to know your *True Personality*. Discipline in its higher form is making small sacrifices in order to obtain a greater good.

Use discipline when you feel lazy. Use discipline and practice meditation rather than return to the superficial pleasures of the past. Use discipline to say a prayer of comfort rather than give in to old fears. Discipline your mind to concentrate on what your heart desires.

The symbols we have given you for inner strength will only work if you have the discipline to use those symbols. The exercises in the book will only work if you have the discipline to perform them. Reading the exercises will do some good, but much more if you are disciplined enough to at least attempt practicing each step. Through your own discipline you will experience the reality of the message of this book.

Be aware that your mind will be distracted. Your thought patterns are still within the vibration of the ego and its fears and worries still linger. Your ego, which has grown so strong throughout the years, will need to be disciplined towards different goals. It will take awhile before the familiarity of the past will no longer tempt you towards the old ways of being. Since the message of this book is foreign to the ego's thought patterns it would not be unusual if some readers find themselves growing sleepy and bored as they try to focus on the words. If the desire within them is strong they will struggle along sentence by sentence, gathering what knowledge they can. That is discipline that grows from true desire.

As you begin to develop discipline as part of your way of being, you should also have patience with yourself. This is not meant to confuse you. Discipline without patience becomes rigid. Patience without discipline can easily become self-indulgence. These two aspects must work together. Do not worry. You will find the balance you need with time and practice.

Patience comes with self-awareness. Only you can determine when patience becomes laziness. Have confidence in your ability to know yourself. Patience will come when you are willing to lose control, when you are aware that knowledge will come when you are ready. Do not try to force yourself to evolve. Patiently wait for those experiences that will come to you and help further your development.

You must also be patient with yourself during times when you fall back into old habits. When you find yourself looking over your shoulder, thinking what you once had is more important than where you are going, be patient. Should you find yourself repeating old patterns of being, should what you thought was finally behind you suddenly reappear stronger than ever, be patient.

You can be patient and forgiving of yourself, but you must also be disciplined so old patterns will last only as long as need be. Be patient and disciplined so your looking to the past will be only a fleeting glance rather than a lingering stare. With discipline you sill learn quickly. With patience you will learn what you need to learn. Do not allow the ego to torment you with false goals and deadlines. Evolution has its own timetable. Spiritual reality is not confined by the restrictions of time and space. You cannot force yourself to achieve a greater awareness. It will unfold in a way that is best for your development. Be aware that the ego will try to control that which is spiritual and such an attempt will only confuse you. The ego must be denied power.

Many readers of this book will be confused, thinking we judge the ego as wrong, thinking we have condemned the ego as something bad. This is not true. We say again the ego is not to be judged. It is only a stage in development, but many who walk the earth are preparing themselves for the next step in human evolution. This book is to remind them of their freedom to choose how they live in the physical realm. Before you can reach a decision you must be aware of the limitations of the ego and know, as well, the reality of the *True Personality*.

You can only expand your awareness and come to experience your spiritual abilities when you have lessened the hold of the ego. When you no longer cherish the ego-image you have of yourself then you will come to know your *True Self*.

You can, if you choose, live your life on earth within the confines of the ego. You will still learn and make some progress. It is a difficult and often painful way, but effective to some degree. It is also a slow way to learn. Learn, if you want, by walking in the way of the ego, but at least try to be open to the experience of spiritual reality. Until then you have never made a choice. You are only repeating what others have taught you. You are only conforming to the way of life that surrounds you. You have given up your true spiritual power.

Every moment of your time on earth you must decide. Do not allow a lazy mind to deny you the chance to experience the force of God in your life. The force we speak of is all around you and within you. You have just not given yourself the chance to experience it.

With patience and with discipline you can open the door to new experiences. You can open the door to experiencing God's love. Once you have felt even a small bit of that love you will not want to return to ego. The limitations of the ego disintegrate in the light of God.

Be aware that the evolution of mankind is at hand. The first step in evolution is the realization of the kingdom of God is within, that you are a spiritual being, so much more than flesh and blood. The door to that realization has always existed. Throughout mankind's existence on earth many individuals have found that door, but it is at this time that many doors are being opened. Many who walk the earth at this time seek that light.

You can open this door. You must decide. There is no reason as to why the door would be beyond your reach. No sin of the past, no crime committed locks the door for all eternity. You have held the key to unlock that door all your life. You came into this world with the key. You may have forgotten it, but have never lost it.

The key to that door is love, a greater love than you have ever experienced. It is a love all yearn for, but seldom seek. It is a love that is real and can be a force in your life if you would only ask for it.

With discipline and patience you will remember the forgotten key of love. When you find it the door shall be opened. Through the door you will find who you truly are. Through that door you will find God.

# Chapter 19

## Peace

Rest now and be at peace. Let go of your worries and fears. Abandon your ambitions. Allow your body the time to relax. Quiet the mind of all questions and opinions. Just be. You have nothing to prove. There is nothing to chase after. Be still. Listen to your heart.

The journey is long. Sometimes it is arduous. Enormous exertion and great concentration is needed as you demolish walls, confront your fears and battle the conflicts that hinder your passage on earth. Evolution, though natural, is sometimes difficult. When you have reached one plateau of understanding you must rest before attempting to conquer new heights.

Throughout the evolutionary journey there will be times of rest, times of quiet repose in which all strivings will come to nothing, all endeavors be futile and even the simplest tasks prove frustrating. During such times your soul, your spiritual energy has turned inward. Even your physical body seeks to be replenished, to gather onto itself needed energy and become revitalized. Therefore, seek solitude and quiet. Keep the tasks of daily life to a minimum. What you do in life matters little. Who you are is everything. Just be who you are; a light in the world, a soul created in love, a force in the universe which needs no reason to justify its existence. It is enough to just exist.

It is only your mind that keeps you from feeling the quiet peace within you. A thousand thoughts, a thousand distractions, a thousand worries fill each day. Always there is something to be accomplished. Always there is a new goal to be reached. Always there is something demanding your attention. Greater care is given to objects, your home or your car, than you give to yourself. Many people show more concern for the dishes in the sink, the dust beneath the chair, the dent in the fender, than they show for their own souls. While the material objects in their lives are given precious attention and lavish care, they themselves are forgotten. Their own spirits remain starving. Their attention is always outward, focused on distractions while their own inner being is ignored.

Consider for a moment the stress and illness that accompanies the neglect of the self. Like all things in nature your energy ebbs and flows. You, as well, have seasons of growth and dormancy. There are times when your actions bear fruit and times when you must rest. There are times you must make great effort to reach beyond your limitations and there are times when you must be still and gather strength. To follow the dictates of the mind with its constant strivings and need to keep busy is to ignore the natural flow of energy within you. This will lead to exhaustion and only hasten the deterioration of the body.

When the physical body is stressed or ill, the ego rises to protect it. Whenever the body is threatened in any way, the ego, being fearful, comes into control. Your thoughts and actions then become limited once again. Your focus is on the physical body; your consciousness is dominated by uncomfortable physical sensations. Spiritual awareness becomes clouded and you deprive yourself of the greater energies and understandings, which can aid in your healing.

Realize and understand that during your present stage of development you are using a physical form in order to learn. Be aware of the body's subtle energy fields, how they flow in you and through you. The body is a perfect and natural receiver and transmitter of energy. Respect it and treat it well. No matter it's condition, no matter what "defects" you perceive as a burden, know your present form will serve you well and there is much to learn within the physical realm of the self.

As your consciousness evolves so will your awareness of the physical self. You will come to recognize the seasons of your own being. You will know when to advance and when to retreat. You will be cognizant of the body's needs, knowing what foods are required, knowing when certain energies need to be adjusted, as well as, knowing and allowing the mind, the body and the emotions to rest.

We ask you now to be at peace. We ask you to be disciplined and put this book away for a day or two before rushing on to the next messages. Take time now to rest. You think reading a book to be a simple task of little effort? If only one new thought has entered your consciousness, if even in a small way you have come to a new understanding, then you have accomplished much more than you realize. Even one single new thought can cause a reaction within you. Every thought is a seed. Given time to grow that one thought can take root and blossom. If, however, you rush about gathering seeds, one new thought after another, that is all you will have, a mind full of seeds, but no fruit.

For a new thought to cause a shift in consciousness it must be given time to grow. It must be nurtured, protected, and allowed to set forth its roots through the various levels of personal energy. It needs to descend from the mental to the emotional and physical vibrations of the self. It needs to become firmly established. Allowed to grow a single thought can bring your entire being into a higher vibration. This shift to a new vibration takes time and sometimes can be uncomfortable. It is not unusual for the physical body to experience a process that is often painful.

As new thoughts and new vibrations begin to grow and shift energies of the body, areas of stagnant energy are loosened and cast off. Though painful, realize it is a process of healing rather than an illness. It is the physical manifestation of purging, a catharsis on the molecular level which allows the physical self to accept new energies of a different vibration. This process can take many forms. In some cases the illness is obviously a physical adjustment as when phantom symptoms suddenly appear and then quickly vanish. In other cases it may appear as any other type of illness and must be treated accordingly, that is, by whatever means are available which will help the body to heal itself.

Certain rituals of a religious nature were used in ancient times specifically as an aid to the physical shift of self-transformation. Rites such as fasting and baptism, the practice of inducing intense sweating, even certain dances were used to help the body cast off stagnant energy. Purification ceremonies do have an effect on the physical body. However, if such actions are done with a limited focus, seeing only its symbolic aspects or performed merely as a routine, then the power of the ritual is diminished. The mental attitude of the participants can conflict with the energies of the ritual. Nevertheless, the physical body will respond to the physical properties of the ceremony even if its power becomes diluted by mental and emotional interference.

On the emotional level there is also a need for purification. Certain emotions of a primitive nature cannot harmonize with the higher vibrations and need to be purged. In such cases old memories and their highly charged emotional attachments will surface. Old fears and pains will be felt again. As these emotions are pushed out of your consciousness and memory they are being cleansed. You will retain the wisdom learned from those painful experiences, perhaps even come to understand why such events have happened in your life, but the power of those lower emotional vibrations will cease influencing your actions on earth. In the past there have also been certain practices to encourage emotional purification. We have given you the most powerful one—forgiveness. Use the tools we have given you. They will help you with each step even when the step you take is painful. Do not fear the suffering and hold the thoughts only in your mind where they can be safely memorized. Changing your thinking is only a small part of growth.

Evolution involves all aspects of your personality. The mental, emotional, and physical aspects are the trinity you can easily distinguish but know that transformation is also taking place on levels of which you are not yet aware. All these different aspects of your personality are being affected and the process can be difficult.

And so we say again, when times of rest present themselves welcome the stillness and peace. Do not allow the mind to fight against "doing nothing." Do not protest. Do not seek to fill every moment of your life with meaningless action. Simply allow yourself the experience of rest. Do not be afraid to be alone with yourself. Remember, you are never alone. As you sit in stillness, as the turmoil and distractions of the world are set aside, spiritual forces gather around you. These forces come to help you make the adjustments, help you to heal and grow. Much can be done in the quiet hours.

For every mountain you have climbed there is another, but in between there are meadows and in such places you can rest. On a bed of grass and wild flowers feel the healing energy of the earth. Gaze calmly at the expansive sky and let all cares and worries drift like clouds in the wind. Feel the warmth of the sun surround and strengthen you. Yes, there is another mountain to ascend. You can see it in the distance. When you are ready you will make the climb. For now be at rest. For now be at peace.

Put aside this book for a day or more, for as long as you like. Return to it when you feel you are ready, when you feel refreshed. Though the mind may urge you onward, be disciplined and deny it's insatiable hunger. It is not enough to merely read words. You must feel the message alive within you, feel it taking root and growing. Know that you have already accomplished more than what is apparent. You have earned the right to rest.

Be at peace.

# Chapter 20

## The Limits of Love

Consider the eagle in its cage. Consider the lion in the circus. Consider the horse harnessed and tethered in its corral. See these images and realize such is love captured by the ego.

That which is majestic, that which is beautiful, that which is powerful the ego tries to cage, tries to tame, attempts to control by imposing boundaries on love's true beauty. Love then becomes an eagle that cannot fly, a lion forced to perform, and a horse that can no longer roam. Still, the eagle will stretch its wings, the lion will roar, and the horse will rear up flailing its hooves: a reminder to all of their true nature.

The soul knows as well its own true nature and so will seek the true power of love. The soul knows it was created in love and will return to love. The soul knows that true love is the highest vibration that can be experienced on earth. This glorious energy of love, this vibration of great magnitude, this eternal power far beyond mere physical sensations, is the life force of the soul. Deprived of this energy the soul will suffer just as the physical body suffers if deprived of air, food, or water. The soul suffers in the world because it cannot find the nourishment it seeks. In a world within the confines of the ego, love has become too small, a teasing glimmer of the sublime power the soul desires.

The ego has taken true love and diminished its potency by romanticizing love into gentle images of hearts, flowers, and sexual innuendo. We remind you again, the ego is concerned with survival and even in love it will seek a mate in accordance with its beliefs of well being even within a romantic context. It will seek a partner of particular attributes the ego has deemed worthwhile. In many cases the ego will even impose virtues on a potential candidate, thereby entering into a relationship with certain expectations. Even romance becomes idealized when the ego begins to demand a standard of behavior from its perspective partner.

The ego begins by looking outward, relying on its physical senses to make a judgment, not only judging physical appearance, but demeanor, survival capabilities, and other specific qualities the ego insists to be important. When two egos come together as possible mates the courtship ritual can become quite elaborate, an interplay of power and pursuit, of openness and guarded trepidation. Each ego enters the courtship ritual in the quest for self-fulfillment. It wants love, but will not give love unless the ego deems it safe to do so.

The ego is so fearful of the liberating power of love, fearful of being vulnerable, that it allows itself to experience love, even the limited romantic love, only if it sees some reward for itself. The ego takes love and makes it a commodity, giving love as a reward and withdrawing love as a punishment. When the demands of the ego are frustrated love is withheld. In this way the ego has taken the universal power of love and limited love to a personal feeling, precious and rare, specific and exclusive.

Some individuals have become so entrapped within their limitation of love that they will only have relationships with individuals they have encountered in previous lives, bringing in "Karmic" confusion to further complicate the relationship. In some cases this is done so individuals can achieve mutual spiritual advancement through several shared existences on earth. When it is a soul-connection forming a relationship on earth, it is true love which binds the individuals in mutual spiritual support, each encouraging the other to evolve.

However, such relationships are rarely of a romantic expression. More often they are parent and child, siblings, friends, and yes, even enemies. It is those relationships that are the most challenging which bring about the greater evolution. Though the ego envisions a relationship of perfect bliss, unconditional love, and sexual compatibility, aspects that are safe and nurturing to the ego, the true love shared by soul mates often presents a more dynamic and demanding relationship. Is it any wonder so many people become disappointed by love?

The ego has an expectation of an ideal love that is safe, a love that does not demand, a love that caters to the ego. Even if such a love did exist, how would it help you evolve?

It would only enforce the power of the ego. It is those relationships that most challenge the ego that will help you evolve. Yet, the ego does not see this as love. It fears that which threatens its existence.

For many other personalities it is this fear that keeps them tied to a particular group of people: reincarnating together and becoming stuck within the self-created energy field of familiarity. Entire cultures have become stagnant due to the insular relationship of its souls. When a culture is forced to change, through invasion by outside forces, or by shifts in natural energies that make their way of life no longer possible, the souls are forced to advance. At this time you can see this occurring with certain courageous Tibetan souls who are reincarnating outside their familiar culture.

As it is with groups of people so it is within families. A smaller culture exists, but is still the same need for familiarity. A core of souls will continue to reincarnate together, taking different roles, forming different relationships, but still remaining within an established connection. This explains why those who marry into such families often feel forced to the perimeter of the family. Such souls who marry into an established group feel themselves to be an outsider, sometimes made to feel as if they were an intruder. Such families emphasize the relationship of "blood" ties, the family above all else. In your present time there is much said about the disintegration of "family values." What is occurring is a shift in consciousness beyond the limitations of a family identity. It is an attempt at liberation from an imposition of an inherited belief system formed by the family. This has happened periodically throughout human history and does precede a shift in awareness. Such transitional periods are difficult and to the ego, quite alarming.

Any action, which challenges the ego's belief system, whether from rebellious youth, or the actions of the great spiritual teachers, causes fear. Because of this fear of change love remains limited. True love, eternal love, the force of God uniting all of creation, has the power to transform. The encompassing vibration of true love goes beyond the self. It cannot be controlled, cannot be manipulated, and cannot be tamed. In the light of this true love, the ego's limited identity fades into shadow.

To the human mind such a power is beyond comprehension and so it settles for less, it settles for a love it can control, a love that is given in the hope of a reward, a love that does not challenge the ego's identity.

The ego has caged love, has forced it to focus on a select group of people be it family, culture, or race. It is because of the ego's limitations that love has become limited. Rather than the experience of love's boundless energy, the ego restricts it to another individual, a small group of familiar souls, or a particular culture. To the ego it is only those who meet its restrictive criteria who are worthy of receiving love.

This restrictive love, this focus on the self in relationship with a particular individual, this attachment to particular groups of race, religion, and culture are the root of all conflict found in the world; families in conflict with outsiders, race suspicious of race, religion in competition with religion, nationalism creating artificial borders. Human consciousness has yet to expand beyond it's own self-identity and therefore creates divisions where divisions do not exist. Since it remains focused outward, lacking a true inner perception of reality, the ego continues to focus on physical differences. In this way it can strengthen its own limited sense of self by creating groups and sub—groups of shared values, be it language, culture, race, religion, or flesh and blood. The ego must then maintain a separation from those outside its self-identity. Separation breeds conflict.

This conflict, produced by the ego's need for self-protection and its limited capacity to love, has reached the stage where humanity has developed the means to destroy itself. By focusing its energies and mental abilities according to the primitive ego, humanity has forsaken wisdom in its pursuit of physical survival. The ego has reached its pinnacle of dominance and change is inevitable—one-way or another.

Mankind will be encouraged to evolve. Those on earth will be pushed to grow beyond their limitations. There are forces at work, which will help individuals take the next step in their evolution. There are forces that will help all of humanity move beyond the stage of ego. We remind you that everything in creation is changing. Such is the nature of the universe. That which ceases to change ceases to exist.

It is not our intention to frighten you. You have enough fears as it is. Why would we add to them? But we speak of these things so that you may have the knowledge. With such understanding you will find the strength to evolve. Knowing that mankind is entering a transitional stage of development will help you face the painful growing pains. It is the purpose of this book to help you find the courage to go beyond a limited love and seek, that which is more powerful than your fears. With this information you may come to realize that an individualized love centered on the self must be relinquished. Though fear of loneliness may intrude, though you may still cling to an image of perfect romantic love, you must realize it is not enough. Those of you who have already lost hope of knowing true love; we encourage you to keep seeking.

Your soul has become restless. It hungers for that which it could not find in the world. It hungers for the nourishment of love, a love without fear, a love given without hesitation. And so you must look elsewhere. You must look beyond the definitions of love given by the ego. You must look beyond the world in conflict. You must search for this love in the heavens. You must search for love in the depth of your own being.

# Chapter 21

▼

# Divine Love

We begin this chapter with an apology. Whatever words we use can only give a glimpse of what exists. The gift we want to give you cannot be expressed in words. The real gift is greater. To truly know of its reality you must discover it for yourself. It must be experienced and it can be experienced if you so desire. We want you to have the experience of Divine Love, to feel for yourself an energy so great, so powerful, so all-encompassing that creation would cease to exist without it.

We cannot give you this love for that would imply it could also be taken away. Divine Love cannot be given as a gift and it cannot be taken away as a punishment. It just is. It is universal and it is personal. It flows throughout creation, giving life to the smallest flower, giving life to you.

This power is eternal. Time cannot destroy it. Space cannot contain it. The power of Divine Love is unconditional. It does not discriminate. It is like the sun that shines on the evil and the good, like the rain that falls on the honest and dishonest alike. This Divine Power, this magnificent energy, this unconditional love exists for all. Nothing in creation is outside its force.

And yet, you do not feel it. Perhaps, you even doubt its existence. You cannot feel it, cannot see it, cannot touch it, therefore it cannot be real. Realize there is much in the universe the human eye cannot see. Even in your own world there are certain wavelengths of light, certain decibels of sound beyond a human's capability to perceive. Still, these higher vibrations of light and sound do exist.

The Divine Love we speak of is real and you will someday experience it for yourself. First you must come to understand what keeps you from truly knowing Divine Love. In the past you were guided by the limited understanding of the ego to look outside yourself for love, to look for the right circumstances, the right time, the right person to bring you love. It is like being far-sighted, looking towards the horizon, unable to see what is so near. That is the way of the ego.

When you came upon the earth you entered a realm of a certain, limited vibration. As we have said the energetic field of ego consciousness is self-contained; its wavelength is short and its vibration is low as it stays close to the physical body as protection. Within the force field of ego consciousness, it is difficult to feel higher vibrations of energy. Since you have grown accustomed to the familiarity of ego vibrations, the higher, more intense energies of what you call a spiritual nature, are not yet recognized. In other words, you have become numb, trusting physical sensations as "real" and other energies as non—existent, or an aberration, or an imaginary phenomenon manifesting itself on the physical level.

Because the mind does not accept unfamiliar energetic vibrations, energies independent of visible cause and effect, powers such as Divine Love are rejected. What is rejected cannot be experienced. A limited consciousness is unable to register the effects of these spiritual powers. The conscious mind has been directed to focus solely on physical vibrations. Spiritual energies are beyond its comprehension. A wall of ignorance blocks spiritual reality.

Because your consciousness, the mental, emotional, and physical aspects of your personality, is directed outward into the physical world you have become sensitive to vibrations of a physical nature. You accept these sensations as reality, the only reality, and continually seek out and accumulate experiences that appease your physical senses.

This is something you were taught to do. As soon as you came upon the earth, while taking on a mortal form within the womb, physical sensation became part of your experience. As your awareness of earth increased you were taught directly and indirectly, by the examples of family and other social interactions, to adjust your personal vibration to the prevailing ego-consciousness. Therefore, understand, the slower vibrations of the ego are not what you would call "natural." Egotistical energy is an adaptation, a harmonizing with surrounding vibrations. You entered the realm of egotistical vibration and were taught the thought patterns, the actions and the emotional responses appropriate to that realm.

What you have learned can be overcome. It is simply acknowledging that there is more to life. We say again and again, there is so much more to creation than the human mind can comprehend. There is so much more you can experience than you have ever known in the past. The universe flows with a numberless multitude of energies, colors, and sounds, each with their own distinct vibration. On earth you have experienced some of these energies through love and anger, fear and hope, pain and joy. You have felt the energies of warmth and cold, of hunger and contentment, of isolation and union. These are familiar to you. They are particular energies of the physical realm with their unique vibrations.

But you are not limited to these vibrations. The human potential is so much greater. Understand that the awareness of mankind is on the verge of expanding to its next level. Humanity is preparing to take the next step in evolution. It has already begun. It has begun with you.

Yes, you who hold this book, you who have been seeking, you who want more out of life, help bring humanity to new understandings. You who have felt different but did not know why, you who found no satisfaction in the pleasures of the world, you who have mourned, you who have felt poor, you who felt denied, yet still you continued to reach out. It is you who will take the next step. It is you who will experience this great power of Divine Love.

All we have given you so far is to help you. We have guided you towards the discovery of greater aspects of reality. As the thoughts presented in this book begin to alter your consciousness and increase your awareness your own personal vibration will change. The exercises given in this book as a gift to you have already begun to transform your energy, as the lower vibration of weakness becomes the more powerful vibration of strength, as the slower energy of sorrow is raised to the higher energy of forgiveness, as the destructive power of hate intensifies to the creative power of compassion.

Strength, forgiveness, compassion are all-powerful. They have an effect in the world. It is just because the world around you still cherishes the ways of the ego that those lower energies are glorified and made to seem more powerful, at times even overwhelming. Remember always, the powers of the ego are limited in capability. They are also short-lived. They are particular energies of the earth, but the earth will change. Mankind will change. It must change. However, the spiritual energies, which are universal and eternal, remain constant. They will remain forever powerful, forever a part of creation, forever a part of you.

The greatest of all these powers we call Divine Love. We call it such so you may understand. We call it Divine Love because it has the power to open the heart. It has the power to awaken your own ability to love. Your own soul pours forth love without fear or hesitation. Broken hearts are healed and sorrow is washed away. Within the experience of this love there can no longer be separation. The unity of all creation is experienced because all of creation is united in this power. Your *True Personality*, your eternal self, your soul and spirit are unveiled by this power and you feel love, true love, and eternal love.

Realize, however, the love you feel comes from your own being in response to the power of Divine Love surrounding you, flowing through you, touching not only your heart, but every cell, every molecule, every atom of your existence. You respond with love. It is a love that exists for its own sake, a natural flow of energy, pure and strong.

But know that Divine Love is so much more. Yes, it is love, but that is only one aspect of its power. It also has the power to awaken your consciousness to new aspects of reality. It has the power to open the heart to its full potential. It can illuminate the mind towards deeper understandings. It can transform weakness into strength. It can impart peace and a sense of well-being.

Know as well that Divine Love can also destroy. Because the intensity of this power increases your own vibration that which is of a lower and weaker energy, that is, the powers of the ego are vanquished. Your own sense of identity takes on a new definition. The old self, the ego self, is diminished. Precious beliefs, cherished prejudices, false judgments fade in the light of Divine love. For many people this power of Divine Love to destroy illusions is too threatening. As we have said in an earlier chapter, and we remind you again, inner conflict is the clash between the lower vibrations of the ego in opposition to the higher and more intense vibrations of spirit. Conflict is the limited self in discord with the eternal vibration of Divine Love. While the ego seeks false security at the expense of personal growth, Divine Love forces all of creation to grow and reach its full potential.

It is like an electrical current that causes a light bulb to fulfill its purpose. Without it, the light bulb is only glass and filament. Without it there is only darkness. It is like the elements of sun, water, and soil helping the seed realize it is a flower. Without it the seed remains only a seed buried in darkness.

So it is with your soul. Without Divine Love it ceases to be. You are light, an eternal light of beautiful brilliance. This light gives life to the body, gives it motion, and gives it expression. This light of the soul is in turn given existence by the powerful energy of Divine Love.

So great is this power that it cannot be fully defined in human terms. Even the words we use cannot adequately describe it. Yet, it can be experienced on earth. Many of those you call saints have known this power, have felt it guiding them even in times of difficulty. Your great spiritual teachers tried to lead their students towards this love. The Master walked the earth so you would know this power, know that it is real, and know that it is yours. The love we speak of is already with you, but you have yet to feel it's full power. It will happen. You have the ability to feel Divine Love. Nothing in the past keeps you separated from this love. You are worthy of experiencing this great power.

Realize dear child, you already have Divine love within you. It is in your possession. The love you seek is within you. It is your own true being, your own *True Self*. It is yours now and forever. Nothing can take it away.

When you finish this chapter give yourself a moment of quiet. Close your eyes, take a few deep breaths and relax. Let nothing disturb you. Do not be bothered by any chores waiting to be done. Let nothing outside you intrude and distract you.

When you are ready concentrate your attention on the center of your chest. Place your right hand there as a point of focus. Breath slowly and deeply. Be aware of any feelings in your chest. If it is uncomfortable or painful or sorrowful, relax and breathe deeply. It will pass. Using your creative abilities envision a bright gold light gathering in your chest. See it expand reaching from shoulder to shoulder, from your neck to your navel. Take as much time as needed. If you can feel its effect, feel the vibration of this light so much the better, if not, be patient. With practice and concentration you will develop the sensitivity to feel different energies. For now it is enough to begin using your creative capabilities to bring energy into your life.

Breath deeply and slowly. Allow the gold light to grow within you, filling you completely. By doing so you begin to look within, awakening to your full potential, realizing your power and abilities as a spiritual force. With this simple exercise you begin experiencing new energies, new vibrations.

In this quiet state, a golden light is within you and around you. If you have the courage, if you are willing to take the next step in your evolution, begin to love. From the center of your chest a light extends out into the world. Send that light to those you know, friends, family and even enemies; those who love you and those who have caused you pain. Extend the light and love even further. Send it into your surrounding area, places you have been, along streets and highways. Then go further, across land and across sea. Extend your love into the world. You have the power to do so. You have the power to bless.

Go even further. From your heart send love into the universe. Let it flow freely to distant stars and planets. Let it be given to those no longer on earth, those who have left the physical realm. Have no fear. This love protects you. This love is powerful. This love is a vital force in creation and it is unending. It flows through you without effort. You only need to be willing.

And, when you have sent love as far as it would go, have it return to the center of your chest. Give this energy of love to yourself. Feel love for yourself. Love the beautiful masterpiece that is you. Love yourself as you are loved. Unless you have this gift for yourself, unless you can love yourself as a vital part of creation, it is impossible to extend this love to others.

This chapter is now over. Take the time to experience the light within you. Bring that light into the world. Now go and use your power.

## Chapter 22

# The Beginning

Soon you will come to the end of this book. You will turn the last page and it may seem as if a door has suddenly closed, then silence. But this is only a book, only words printed on paper. These words are only a communication between realms. We, who once dwelled upon earth and now are part of what you call the spiritual realm, have spoken to you. All is the spiritual realm. There is no separation, only differences. We have not spoken of how our realm differs from yours. Such things are unimportant. It is the message that is important, not the messenger.

We have communicated with you because we are aware of your particular struggles on earth. Our awareness extends beyond our realm to include other realms, other manifestations of creation as well. Many of us have walked the earth. We have known the experiences of having a physical body. We know of its joys and sorrows. We have felt the love and the fear. We have struggled. We have had our teachers to help us. Earth is a part of us and we remain a part of earth as all of creation is from the same source. All of creation is worthwhile. Some of us have chosen to return and as you read these words are preparing to come again upon the earth for there is much wisdom to be gained in your realm. It is a place of wonderful learning.

Therefore, we know of what we speak. We have experienced the message. We know its difficulties and we know its rewards. We only wish to share what we have learned through experience and that will be our final message for this book.

Experience life. It is your path on earth that will teach you.

These few words are only a guide. If you have accepted the message of this book then already your awareness has grown and you have taken the next step in your evolution. Or perhaps acceptance is still in the future. Perhaps the thoughts presented to you are still in conflict with old thought patterns. Be patient. Consider the words, test the message, and seek the experience of truth. Listen to your feelings. Listen to your soul. Do not be so quick to reject new possibilities. We already know that not all who read this book will be in agreement. Some people may even be angered. So be it.

We offer this message as a gift, one given in love. Whether or not it is accepted is of little concern. We give it to you and ask nothing in return. We do not even ask that you believe in us. We ask you believe in yourself. Believe that you are so much more than the world would have you think. Believe that you are eternal, that you are a beautiful expression of divine creativity, a masterpiece of creation loved and cherished.

Believe we are always with you. Even when this book has ended we remain with you. It is only the ego that believes itself to be alone, which believes it must be a power unto itself. The ego's perception of isolation is limited awareness.

Understand that there is no separation between realms. Energy flows freely between worlds, between different realities. Your personal vibration becomes attuned to energies of a similar vibration. There is always an interplay of harmonizing vibrations. Lower vibrations will attract experiences and be influenced by powers of a lower vibration. The clearer, brighter vibrations of an individual will draw to it the influences of corresponding vibrations. Negative will attract negative. Positive will attract positive. Sorrow will attract sorrow. Hatred attracts hatred. Love begets love. Light unites with light and where light exists there can be no darkness.

Remember, evolution is more than new ideas. It is more than what you think. It is how you feel, how you walk in the world, how your individual energy emanates in the universe. Though the words of this book come to an end, the message will remain, like a seed awaiting the proper time to grow. You will keep it inside you. When the time is right it will come forth. Meanwhile, just by reading the message, your vibration has been altered. For many readers it will be impossible to turn back. For others the next step may not be taken in this lifetime, but there will be other opportunities. When desire is strong within you the message will be remembered.

And we will be always be with you, reminding you of its existence, reminding you there is more to life. We will stay with you and love you no matter what decisions you make. Even if you reject the message, even if you ignore us, still we remain by your side. Because we are patient. Because we have hope. Because we love you.

We will keep giving our gifts. There will be other messages to help you on your journey. When you are ready to accept new knowledge the message will be waiting for you. Realize, however, that we have more to offer than mere words. When you put away this book you set aside one gift and are then ready to receive others.

When you have reached the last page, when you are able to sit quietly without distraction, we will impart our wisdom, our strength, and our love. You only need to be open to receive it. You only need to feel it surround you and flow through you. We will help as much as we can to raise your vibration, to expand your awareness, to help you remember the beautiful light of your soul. When we can we will help heal you. When we can we will protect you. We will do what we can to help you discover your own power, your own abilities, and your own potential as a spiritual being walking the earth.

We cannot, however, keep you from your lessons. You will still struggle and grow. You will still face challenges. We have never promised a safe and trouble—free existence on earth. That is what your ego seeks. It hungers for a guarantee it will survive. It follows those who promise wealth, security, health, and long life. Those are the desires of the ego. That is the quest of a consciousness bound by physical reality.

We speak to your soul. We speak to your *True Self*. We remind you of your potential to learn, grow, and evolve beyond the limitations of physical reality. We speak as well to your temporal self; you who have chosen to walk the earth, you who have chosen to partake of physical experiences. Though we could not and would not take away the unique challenges you face in the realm of physical reality, we do offer you tools to help you on the journey. We also walk by your side giving our support and encouragement as you take the next difficult step.

And so the book will end but for you it is a beginning. You will put the book aside, perhaps forget it exists, and perhaps forget the message itself. It is, after all, only a stepping-stone. It is time to move on. A door has opened and now you must step through and see what life has to offer. It has much to give you. Be not afraid.